Like Mother, Like Daughter?

The effects of growing up in a homosexual home

Jakii Edwards with Nancy Kurrack

Like Mother, Like Daughter?
by Jakii Edwards with Nancy Kurrack

Printed in the United States of America
ISBN 1-931232-44-X

Xulon Press
344 Maple Ave. West, #302
Vienna, VA 22180
703-691-7595
XulonPress.com

Dedication

To my mother, Dorothy, whom I came to love with all my heart

***

To my brother, Reggie, who lived with me through the holocaust of growing up with Dorothy

***

To my children, Durksen and Scott, who had to live with me through my healing from the effects of life with Dorothy

Foreword

I have known Jakii Edwards for over ten years and have had the opportunity to be her pastor. We preachers often say, "Your test will be your testimony; your mess will one day be your message." This rings true for Jakii. Her life has given her a testimony and a message that needs to be heard.

Her mother, who was a lesbian, raised Jakii in the 1950s. Jakii's childhood experiences give her the authority and expertise to speak about homosexuals raising children and the subsequent effects. Though her childhood was filled with abuse, she describes eloquently what issues every child who is raised by homosexual parents will go through, whether raised in a loving environment or a troubled one. Through the years she has helped many children and adult children of homosexual parents deal with such issues as gender identity problems, emotional insecurities, and peer rejection.

Years after being raised by a lesbian mother, Jakii found the one thing that could put her shattered life and childhood back together: she encountered the one true God. The Lord did more than "give her beauty for ashes, the oil of joy for mourning and a garment of praise for the spirit of heaviness." He raised her up to speak change to thousands of lives.

Pastor Dick Bernal, Senior Pastor/Founder
Jubilee Christian Center, San Jose, California
June 2001

Table of Contents

Preface

Homosexuality today is no longer a "don't ask, don't tell" topic. It's "out-of-the-closet" in headline-making style. Award-winning films and television programs are designed to acclimate a new generation of Americans to the idea that homosexuals are people who make "different" choices for their lives. Many states are busy deciding which benefits and perks to offer homosexual partnerships, and if the American Civil Liberties Union has its way, one state will lead the pack in offering a marriage contract to same-sex couples. These things I personally cannot change.

However, I was raised by a lesbian, and I can speak with authority on one of the most important dilemmas Americans will face and be accountable for in the twenty-first century. If gays and lesbians have the legal right to adopt and form family units, what effects will the homosexuality have on their children?

While in my teens, and as a young woman, I believed all gay women treated their children badly because my mother, Dorothy, was my only frame of reference. I have come to know better, so please understand that my purpose in writing this book is not to infer that all homosexual men and women rear their children in the same manner I was raised.

The Constitution of the United States gives adults the right to make choices for their lives, whether they are right or wrong. My book, therefore, does not address the question of the morality of homosexual behavior. The sole purpose in telling my story is to shed light on the plight of children who are raised in gay or lesbian homes. What do the children feel when they see mommy and mommy kissing, or daddy and daddy coming out of the bedroom hugging each other when their friends are visiting?

This topic has never officially been discussed and stories such as mine, to my knowledge, have never been published. The truth is, very few outsiders really know what goes on behind closed doors in these "different" households. Does Congress, or anyone else making legal decisions, ever investigate the hardships and mental anguish suffered by the children?

Other ills in our society are investigated. The U.S. government has statistics on the number of families in this country, which have been raised by generational welfare recipients. Why is this chain of support difficult to break? Research shows that the lifestyle of living on welfare is learned behavior. First the grandmother, mother, and then the third and fourth generations of single parents almost always end up depending on welfare. It is learned behavior.

The medical community has documented cases of third and fourth generation alcohol abuse in families. How does this happen? Once again, heavy drinking is usually picked up by family members who have been watching a mom, dad, brother, grandfather or Uncle Billy, who regularly drowns his or her sorrows into oblivion. It is learned behavior.

There are also families of third and fourth generation doctors, lawyers, or mechanics. Consider the Petty family with generations of race-car drivers. The tendency for people to pattern after their elders is part of human nature. Therefore, children tend to follow in the footsteps of their parents or the people who raise them. Children raised by homosexuals are not exempt from this phenomenon.

This is a topic I am more than qualified to address, and I've paid a great price to speak and write about these matters. It has taken a tremendous amount of work and time to fight for my healing, to gain my self-worth, and to learn how to emotionally interact with the opposite sex. Specifically, I've had to learn to interact properly with men in the various roles of friendship and romance.

I grew up afraid that one day I would turn into a lesbian. Why? It seemed all the neighborhood kids and their mothers expected me to end up like my mother and they kept telling me so. The amount of anger I built up towards Dorothy was immeasurable. All I ever really wanted was a mom to whom I could talk and a mother who would be like the other moms.

Now I realize that I am not the only child who has lived through this ordeal and has come through with deep scars. I can recall two others.

The first victim was a teenage girl who my oldest son dated during his sophomore year of high school. Let's call her Annie. She always tried to be nice, but I could see the anger and shame she carried inside of her. Annie always wore too much makeup for such a young, pretty girl. Her blouses were usually very low-cut and the principal would have to send her home at least twice a week to change clothes.

What disturbed me most was Annie's reputation in school. She was labeled as an "easy lay" and she had supposedly slept with all the guys. My heart went out to her. One day, when she stopped by to pick up my son, I had an opportunity to ask her why she appeared so sad all the time. Annie dropped her head and mumbled a few unintelligible sentences. I told her about my own experience being raised by Dorothy. I explained that I had gone through a stage when I needed to prove to myself that I was not gay like my mother.

I'll never forget the look of surprise on her face. Annie opened her mouth to speak, but instead she burst into tears, then she turned and ran out of the house. I felt bad for saying anything. About two or three weeks later, my son came home from school announcing that he and Annie had a huge fight in the hall. Both of them had been expelled for the day.

We didn't hear from her for awhile, and then one day Annie's grandmother surprised me with a telephone call. She explained Annie's father was gay and he and his lover lived together. Every other weekend she had to stay with them and she always had a hard time being there. Annie's mother had left her with her grandmother because her father had deserted them.

Annie didn't like the arrangement with her father because even when she spent time over at his house, he would spend most of his time with his male lover. Her grandmother felt that Annie slept with boys to prove she was not gay, and that every time she returned from visits with her father, her bad behavior would increase.

Although Annie liked my son, she admitted she had problems knowing how to talk with guys and interact appropriately with them. She loved her dad but could not cope with his lifestyle because she was ashamed of his actions. It was hard for her to watch her dad and his male lover hugging and kissing in front of her and then going into their bedroom every night.

Annie invited me to her home one day. She and her grandmother sat down and talked about her activities and her visitations with her father. Annie explained that, although her room was down the hall, she still heard the noises they made at night. Annie claimed she cried herself to sleep most nights when she was with her dad.

Later I met her grandmother, and she shared with me that the talks I had with Annie seemed to have helped. Finally, she had found someone who could relate to the confusion and hurt she was experiencing. I often wonder how she's doing now.

The second child was a four-year-old girl who lived with her "butch" mother whom we will call Rachael. I was managing a salon where her mom had her hair done, and every time I saw the family, her mom was usually dressed in either army fatigues or men's pants, masculine shirts, and a man's hat. Her partner was similar in attire although she did not have the exaggerated male walk. These women owned their own business, and between them they had four children. Three were angry little boys, and then there was this little jewel of a girl.

One day when I was working on Rachael's hair, she started talking about how her little girl, Katie, was driving them all crazy. She claimed Katie was guilty of asking for nail polish, lipstick, and jewelry. The little girl was sitting nearby as we talked.

"Now Katie wants a perm!" Rachael reported with a long sigh. "I just don't know where she gets all of that girly stuff. Certainly not from me or Maxine!"

I studied Katie as we talked. She was a fighter and I felt like I could see into her spirit. She was fighting to maintain her femininity despite all the masculinity around her. I managed to sit and talk to her as she was getting her hair cut. Because I could relate to her inner conflicts, I had to ask her why she wanted curls.

"Because I just feel so pretty when my mom has time to curl my hair," she answered.

Her mother overheard our conversation. "Doesn't she just drive you crazy with that curly hair talk?" Rachael interjected. "Every time she goes to her grandma's house she comes back with a baby doll and another *Seventeen* magazine. I swear, why would any four-year-old want to look at *Seventeen*? She can't even read yet and she wants us to read it to her!"

Inside I couldn't help but cheer on that little girl in her battle for her own identity.

Children never seem to have a say in how they are raised or treated. Unless someone who has been raised by same-sex parents or brought up in a lesbian/gay environment speaks out, people will never know what goes on in our private lives. Rarely are these children asked how they feel when mommy kisses other women, or what they go through when daddy is hugging and kissing other men. From a child's perspective, these scenes can be very painful. Whether the gay parents want to own up to their children's feelings or not, the fact remains that they endure pain.

No one feels the agony of your victimization as you do. Each victim has his or her tolerance level, and when that line of pain and suffering is crossed, there is no telling what that person will do in order to survive. Some choose suicide as a way out of the pain. Many children run away (emotionally or literally) as their means of escape. As for me, I dove headlong into a mental shutdown mode which lasted over twenty-five years.

At a very young age I began blocking out as many feelings as possible. As an adult, I eventually had to allow myself to look at those painful years and work through the pain and denial. I did it successfully with the help of the Lord and godly counselors who were sent my way.

After years of ministering to other victims, I found myself being featured on national television programs and several radio talk shows. Everywhere I was interviewed, someone wanted to read my book. At that time I had no book!

One day I received a call from a producer named Nancy

Kurrack who had been assigned to do a feature story on my life. She also felt there should be a book, and after the television story aired, I asked her to help me do the writing.

When Nancy began to ask me to express my feelings about my life with Dorothy, I discovered I couldn't handle it. After all I had been through with my mother, it was very hard for me to express my feelings about my life as the child of a lesbian. I was mad at Nancy for asking me to look deeply into my past to explain every detail about key experiences.

For example, I told Nancy about the terrifying experience which is described in the opening scene of chapter one. "How did you feel the night you heard your mother having sex with another woman?" Nancy probed. "They were in the same bed where you and your brother were sleeping."

"Why doesn't she simply take a hammer and hit me in my chest?" I wondered. I opened my mouth to respond, and only tears came. Now I wanted to deny that anything like that had ever happened. The twelve-year-old girl from my past was confused and frightened by the noises she heard that night; now that I was in my fifties, I still felt the same way. I wasn't ready to give anyone the details. As much as I needed Nancy's help, I still didn't want to reveal all those secrets.

As we continued with the book, I realized that I have lived the majority of my life in a world void of that painful word called "feelings." To feel was like having surgery without the benefit of anaesthetic! Who needs that?

Still, I had to put my feelings to work when learning how to love and show affection for my own children. That may sound silly, but I never received any tenderness from Dorothy, so I didn't know how to show love and affection to others. It took a lot of effort to learn.

For many of you, this will not be an easy book to read. Some of you may even doubt that everything I report is true. Believe me, I could never make up a story like this. Dorothy was a one-of-a-kind mother!

If you are reading this book because you have a child or grandchild living in a gay parental situation, please understand that not all gay parents are anything like my mother. Nevertheless, there is always a certain amount of shame and gender identity questions which linger in our hearts and minds.

We constantly wonder if we will eventually become gay. There is humiliation when other kids see our parents kissing a same-sex lover in front of us. Trust me, it's hard on the children, no matter how much they love their gay parent. The homosexual community may never admit it, but the damage stemming from their actions can be profound.

Possibly you are interested in a healing for yourself or loved ones. I've learned that no one will die from looking back and walking through the pain. On the contrary, with God's help, there is healing and restoration for those who commit to the greatest physician and counselor the world has ever known—Jesus.

I pray that in the telling of my own experiences, much needed light will be shed on the consequences of being raised in a homosexual home and environment. The story that follows includes events which took place during many traumatic days in my past, and one particular night in my childhood stands out as a place for me to begin . . .

Chapter 1

First Clue

Pittsburgh, Pennsylvania. . . Autumn of 1955

I awoke with a start to the sounds of moaning and heavy breathing. The noises were obviously coming from someone lying very close to me in the bed where I was sleeping. Terror gripped my body, and I was not about to open my eyes to see who it was! As a twelve-year-old, I knew this was not just another bad dream. The bed was moving and the sounds were slightly muffled, but most assuredly they were real.

What should I do? I frantically asked myself. My mind was reeling. My first response was to run, but I wasn't even sure where I was. Instead, I decided to freeze in position to keep from drawing attention to myself. *If the person knows I'm awake, whoever he or she is, I'll be in more danger,* I predicted. So, for what seemed like an eternity, I continued to lie in a paralyzed state and tried to remember what had happened earlier that evening.

The cold room was my first indication; my covers had been tossed to the side. I was freezing, but everything started coming back to me from the previous evening. My four-year-old brother and I were spending the night at Carrie's second-floor flat.

Carrie was one of our mother's "special" friends. Even though Reggie and I preferred the security of our grandparents' home, there were occasions when we had no choice but to stay with our mother, Dorothy. We never knew which one of her "friends" she would be staying with or what our living conditions would be like. My grandmother did not mind having us stay with her, but sometimes she would be so furious with Dorothy that she would kick out all three of us.

That's exactly what happened yesterday afternoon, I gradually recollected. Our grandmother had scolded Dorothy for not showing up for three weeks to check in on us, so we were out of the protection of her house again. Tonight we were in Carrie's double bed in her one-room flat. It was a large, rectangle-shaped room. The part which served as the kitchen was simply furnished with a chrome and Formica table. The double bed was at the opposite side by the window.

Around nine o'clock that evening Reggie and I had settled under the covers at the foot of the bed. I could see the streetlight shining through the frosted windowpane. It had reminded me that at least we were still on South Euclid Avenue, just a few blocks down from our grandparents' house. It could have been worse. Sometimes Dorothy stayed with women clear on the other side of Pittsburgh.

Reggie, I panicked. *Is he still beside me?* My mind was screaming, but I did not dare let the words be heard. In fact, my heart was pounding so loudly that I was afraid the noise would give me away. Very carefully I reached out my hand to my left. *Yes, Reggie is still here. Lord, don't let him wake up!* I mentally prayed. I didn't want him to know the terror I felt.

The moaning was getting louder and the bed seemed to be rolling. In my hysteria, every sound seemed to be magnified a thousand times. No matter how hard I tried, I could not make sense of what I was hearing. I couldn't remember anything from my past to compare with this experience.

Now the bed was really moving! Someone's skin brushed up against me, probably a leg, I guessed. It was swaying strangely to the rhythm of the moaning. I tried desperately to lie still and breathe normally as if I were still sleeping. At least, whoever it was did not seem to notice me or care that my brother and I were in the way.

Who else is in this bed with us? What's really going on? As these questions tormented my mind, I heard someone speak in a low, breathy tone.

"Dot . . . Dot!" A female voice was slowly whispering my mother's name over and over again.

Suddenly it became painfully obvious. The sounds had to be coming from both Dorothy and Carrie! Of course, there was only one bed for the four of us. Their heavy breathing and loud moaning now filled the room. *So, just what are they up to?* I wondered, with this new twist in the mystery. Somehow I knew that whatever they were doing was something I did not want to see.

No matter what was going on, I was a captive to the bed. *How long will this last?* was another burning question. I had nowhere to go to escape their dreadful deed and no one to tell.

Hatred for my mother became the only emotion I could feel. Other emotions had long since been shut down from other horrors my mother had put me through. As I continued to lie there with my eyes tightly shut and my breath still, I couldn't help thinking about how Dorothy had shattered my perfect world six years ago.

Chapter 2

The Dethroning
of a Princess

An Upper-middle Class Suburb of Pittsburgh, Pennsylvania. . .
1944 - 1950

"Jakii, come in and see what your Daddy made for you today!" A voice summoned me from the back door of my "real" home.

In a few seconds I scaled down the lower branches of my favorite tree in our back yard to see what all the excitement was about. Back then I had a mother and a father who loved me beyond measure and called me "Princess."

I was a tomboy at heart and loved to wear my coveralls and climb trees. There were days, however, when I insisted on wearing dresses. Not just any dress would do; I had a favorite blue dress with lots of ruffles that I always wanted to wear to school. My dark brown hair was very thick, and I wore it either in curls or three big braids. Two of the braids hung down the middle of my back, and the other one was always in my way because it wouldn't stay to the side of my face where it belonged.

Thomas and Rita Williams had a big, beautiful home in an impressive section of Pittsburgh, and there was enough love between them to ease any problem that might come my way. Actually, no problem back then seemed significant, except "Jell-O."

"Now, Jakii," Mother Williams coaxed in pleasant but firm tones, "that Jell-0 is not going to hurt you. Go ahead and put it in your mouth." I should have been delighted with Jell-0, but I wasn't convinced.

"No, Mommy, it's shaking and I'm afraid." Somehow I would eventually muster up the courage to take a bite with Mom and Dad's encouragement. Then, on other occasions, I would create a scene by holding food in my mouth and refusing to swallow. I know I tried their patience, but how I loved them. I can't remember any "real" problems during the five years I lived with the Williams.

Daddy Williams was a wonderful father. He had a habit of wearing plaid shirts, had a short and sturdy build, and his face was warm and trusting. He didn't laugh a lot, but he always had a pleasant smile. His hair was closely trimmed and he sometimes had a slight beard which tickled me when I hugged him. He was one of the most devoted and generous people I'd ever known.

I love to remember how Daddy would build and carve special toys for me and the other two children in the house. He was always going out of his way to meet our every need. Margaret, Tommy and I especially adored the table set that he built for us. Each of us had our own chair painted our favorite color, and a section of the table was painted in our color, too. My color was pink. We even had special cocoa cups to match. Daddy worked hard in the steel mill five days a week, and although he was tired when he got home, he never stopped trying to make our lives better.

One time Mom wanted a second staircase put in the kitchen so she could get to us quicker when we were sick in bed. Before she could even finish explaining what she had in mind, Daddy was taking measurements so he could knock out walls and get it done. He was that kind of man.

My mother, Rita Williams, stood out among all the other black mothers in our neighborhood, and I was very proud of her. Now I realize she had gone to college and was an excellent teacher. She read wonderful stories to me and taught me to pronounce the letters of the alphabet and to count. I remember how pleased she was when I began to write some of my letters and add sums before I entered kindergarten. Soon I was reading on my own, and she always insisted I use proper English instead of slang.

I often saw Daddy hug my mother and tell her how wonderful she was. She faithfully prepared his breakfast every morning and packed his lunch at four in the morning. On Sundays she baked homemade rolls and bread for him to take to work during the week. We always went to church, and sometimes Mom would stop by the pastor's house on the way to the store just to visit with his wife. We never minded because the pastor's back yard was a great place to play.

Mom was wonderful to all three of us. She put up fruit, pickles and jelly during the summer and fall, and she always baked homemade treats that filled the house with a sweet and wonderful smell. When she was making bread she would let us shape a few pieces of dough into rolls and place them in the pans for baking, and we couldn't wait to eat our own creations. And her creation of homemade cake batter always meant we got to lick the bowl!

Our mom would even take time out of her busy day to play outside with the three of us. A tall wooden fence enclosed our spacious back yard, and there was plenty of room to ride our tricycles or to jump rope. In the afternoons we took naps, and when we got up Mom would serve us cocoa or juice and some sort of snack at our own little table.

In the evening when Mom was cleaning up after supper, Daddy would swing with the three of us on the back porch glider and tell some great stories. Sometimes he made them up; once in a while he recalled incidents from his own childhood. If he happened to fall asleep after telling his tales, Margaret and I would tickle him to wake him up. We knew he would pretend to be a bear and growl at us, and our response was always to run giggling into the house and hide our faces in Mommy's apron.

In the winter we were allowed to play in the basement if it was raining or snowing. However, I loved the snow, and they would bundle me up in snow pants so I could play to my heart's desire. I remember wearing my green coat with a brown fur collar, a fur muff to keep my hands warm, and of course a fur hat to match! As far as favorites go, it came in a close second to my blue ruffled dress.

I was living a fairy-tale life, which made the events that transpired on Valentine's Day back in 1950 so much harder for me to bear. I was five years old and the day was progressing as usual. I knew Mom would be thrilled because I had made her a special gift in kindergarten that morning. I offered it to her the moment I pranced through the kitchen door wearing my fancy blue dress. It was a clay print of my hand.

As usual, the smell of fresh baked cookies filled the kitchen. But to my dismay Mommy had big tears in her eyes when she saw me. I could tell she had been crying for a long time as she slowly ran her fingers across my small clay hand print and tried to smile. "Are you crying because of my gift?" I asked, looking deep into her red and swollen eyes for an explanation.

"Jakii, darling, do you remember what your social worker has been telling you all along? Your Daddy and I are only your foster parents, and someday you'll have to leave us and go to live with your birth mother." Her words were barely audible because of her sobbing. "That day is finally here," she whispered and then took a deep breath.

I knew very well what she was talking about. However, I honestly thought that because my social worker had been killed in a car accident a year ago, the things she had been trying to explain to me had died with her. Of course, I never wanted to believe her no matter how many times she repeated the cold facts. It was her job to get it through to me that I was a foster child. She informed me that a woman named Dorothy Edwards, who sometimes dropped by to visit me, was my real mother.

I had never been impressed with this Dorothy person. She was short and stocky, her dark hair was shoulder length and she always dressed in what looked like men's slacks. She did not seem to be interested in me, either. In fact, I preferred it when her sisters Roberta and Ruthie came to see me. They wanted to know all about me and I had fun visiting with them.

I had settled on the fact that everything Dorothy and her sisters told me was really just a lie. In fact, I had it all figured out in my mind. If I refused to believe the social worker, then what all of them were trying to tell me wouldn't be true.

As far as I was concerned, there was only one problem with my plan. I was afraid I had somehow caused the social worker's death! The last time she had visited I remembered thinking to myself, *Good. I'm glad she's leaving and I hope she never comes back!* That guilt weighed heavily on my five-year-old conscience. Now, it seemed all my plans had failed.

Most of the conversation I had with Mommy that afternoon in the kitchen is now hard for me to remember. As we cried and hugged each other, I could see that someone was waiting around the corner in the living room. Sure enough, there was a man and a woman and they already had my bags. Mommy told me she had to pack them quickly while I was at school. Somehow I had to try some last-ditch effort to keep my world the way I wanted it.

"I promise I'll never do anything wrong again if you just keep me," I frantically pleaded.

I remember grabbing hold of Mother William's skirt and thinking I would never let her go. Mom's loving tones blended with her tears as she tried to help me understand.

"Princess . . . your Daddy and I have done everything possible to keep you with us." She let out a big sob before she could continue. "We would keep you with us forever if we could. It's just that the court has made its decision, and that decision can't be changed."

My final protesting was in vain. The woman named Dorothy, and a man I had never seen before, were the two people in the living room waiting for me. I refused to even look at Dorothy, but it stood out in my mind that the man was tall, slender, and well-dressed in a black coat, black hat and white silk scarf. I did not know it at the time, but he was my great-uncle who had come along with Dorothy to make sure the mission was accomplished. They talked with Mother Williams for a while, but in less than an hour I was forced to leave the only home I had ever known.

Chapter 3

200 South Euclid Avenue

I was in shock. No other word can describe the sensation. I don't remember how the man and woman got me into their car, but I know it was a short drive. It only took about fifteen minutes for them to pull up in front of a large brick house, but how I acted or what they said to me is all a painful blur. I simply wanted to disappear out of their sight.

I no longer belong to the people who love me, was the thought that stabbed my heart. It was definitely a sobering, life-stopping pain. There was one thing that I remember very clearly. On this nightmare of a day, I firmly resolved that the woman named Dorothy would never take my mother's place.

The car pulled to a stop in front of their imposing, three-story red brick house. The address read "200 South Euclid Avenue." Compared to the Williams' beautiful home, this one appeared cold and unfriendly. My thoughts went wild. *This can't be the house where I'm supposed to live!*

The first thing that struck me was the long flight of steps

leading from the sidewalk to the front yard. They seemed to go up forever. Dorothy and the strange man led the way. Once I made it to the landing, I saw a walkway that split in two directions. The main walkway led to another set of stairs which ended on the concrete front porch, and the smaller path curved to the left leading to the neighbor's house and another path between the two houses.

The sun was brightly shining on the frozen yard, but I noticed there were not any trees for such a huge house. Nothing about the old brick house seemed inviting. Four more steps took me up to the gray front porch. Although I was numb with anger and fear, my heart was pounding out of control as I was led to the front door.

The massive double doors were made of dark wood, and the unidentified tall thin man in black opened them for me to enter. I was led through a small vestibule with a mailbox, and then through another door which led into a large entry hall. It was almost big enough to be a room, and it even had an old couch in it. I was quivering! My hands hung to my side and my head bowed low. I was afraid to look around, but I did. The main feature of the entry hall seemed to be the grand staircase leading to the second floor, but I was directed to go through the wooden, sliding double doors on the left which led into a living room.

Lots of people were there waiting for me. I realized they were staring at me, although through my downcast eyes they appeared to be a blur. Dorothy was the first to break the awkward silence. "Here she is!" she announced as she dramatically swept her arms in my direction. "She cried and acted up at the Williams' house and wouldn't even talk to us in the car," she had to add for the desired effect.

Now everyone was definitely glaring. Pointing her finger at

me, she ordered, "Go and say hello to your grandmother!" With that introduction, she roughly pushed me farther into the room. My feet were as heavy as lead.

The tension of the moment was broken as my grandmother walked toward me with warm eyes and a loving smile. She was a tiny lady, but well built and extremely attractive. She, too, had very fair skin similar to mine, and her long dark brown hair was neatly tied back in a bun with a stylish roll on the sides. My grandmother was wearing an A-line wool skirt and a pretty sweater. Instantly I saw her as someone who could give me hope in the midst of a desperate situation. She gently took my right hand into hers and introduced herself. "Hi, I'm your grandmother Alma Edwards, but you can call me Grandmere."

Then she led me to someone who had also caught my attention. One of his legs was a different color than the rest of his body. "Jacqueline, this is your granddad, Robert Glen. Everybody calls him 'R.G.'"

There he was sitting in his big high-back chair to the right of the mantel. Definitely the focal point of the room, he was very busy reading the newspaper and listening to his baseball game on a brown Philco radio. I didn't know how he managed, but he was chewing tobacco and smoking a cigar at the same time. I knew this was true because I saw him spit into a galvanized bucket positioned to the side of his chair and ottoman.

R.G.'s cigar smoke collected into a dirty white cloud which floated to the top of the high ceiling. What a rancid contrast to the delicious aroma of the Williams' home! He appeared to be a big man and was well-dressed with classy suspenders. He peered at me for a second through his wire-rimmed spectacles and grunted something.

Was that a hello? I wondered. To avoid looking at R.G., I studied the pictures on the mantel. My eyes followed the room around to the dark blue velveteen sofa which was positioned on the other side of the room in front of a large picture window. There was no rug on the hardwood floor and no curtain framing the window. Even though the shade was pulled up to allow in the light, the room was still dark and drab.

I was never quite sure who the other people in the room were, even though Grandmere introduced them to me. It seemed they were boarders who rented the extra bedrooms in the big, old house. Grandmere explained that the house had a total of eight bedrooms, including a complete living unit on the third floor.

It didn't take long to discover that Dorothy had more siblings than just the two sisters who had visited me at the Williams' home. While I was still standing with Grandmere in the living room, Uncle Raymond came home from school. He was a tall, lanky twelve-year-old with dark curly hair and a laughing smile.

"Do you like cowboy guns?" he wanted to know. "You can play with mine if you want to." Uncle Ray at least tried to make me feel comfortable. I thought I saw a little twinkle in his eye and figured that he must be mischievous.

Before Uncle Ray finished speaking, my Aunt Roberta burst into the room. She greeted me with, "Hi, kid!" and a big smile. I recognized her as one of the family members who had visited me at "my" house. She was only ten years old, the closest in age to me, and everyone called her Bert. She asked Grandmere if she could give me a tour of the house. My mind was thinking "survival," and I was looking at Bert as someone to play with.

As Bert led me back into the vast entryway, we stopped at the foot of the towering staircase. A large carved lion's head was mounted on the banister, and the dark wooden railing leading to the top was rather wide.

"This is the best part of the house," Bert proudly reported.

"The slide down is really fast, and the lion stops us real good!" Things were looking up. "We're not supposed to do it, but it's great fun!" she added. Together we began the long trek up the stairs, and once on the second-floor landing, I saw a long hallway with many doors.

Bert never stopped talking, "Our bedroom is straight ahead." From what I could tell, it was the room directly above the living room, and it was huge. There were three large windows, two double beds, and several dresser drawers spread throughout the room. There were no pretty pink bedspreads or curtains, and the hardwood floors were bare. The windows held the same pull-down shades I had seen downstairs.

"This is your bed," Bert pronounced as she pointed to the one in the corner. She spent quite a bit of time rattling off all the things that were off-limits to me. Then she ran to one of the dresser drawers and pulled something out. "And this is Ruthie's scrapbook. We're not supposed to touch it!" she explained excitedly as she thrust it toward me. She even helped me turn the pages. Inside were pictures of Rock Hudson, Gary Cooper, Jane Russell, Susan Hayward, and Veronica Lake. "These are Ruthie's favorites!" Bert proudly announced. I was hoping that Aunt Ruthie would not walk in on us and find that we had invaded her privacy.

Bert wanted to know who I liked at the movies, but I had no idea what she was talking about because the Williams had never taken me to the cinema. Thankfully, she kept talking and I didn't have to answer. "We all share this closet," she explained as she opened the door. I saw clothes everywhere: at the top, on hangers, and on the floor.

In my bedroom at my own house my mom always kept my clothes hung up neatly and my room clean. This one was a disaster area. I continued to study the room as Bert rattled on.

There were no bedspreads, curtains or blinds, and it was missing wallpaper, too. Maybe that was why the room seemed so drab even though the windows flooded it with light.

The tour continued down the hallway. Bert explained that all the boys stayed in the room next to ours, and the other two bedrooms were rented out. There was one bathroom for all of us on the floor. I guessed I would no longer have my own color-coded and personalized bath towels. At the other end of the second floor hallway was another stairway leading up to the third-floor flat. "We can't go up there," Bert explained. "Another family lives there." Besides, the door was locked. According to Bert, it had three bedrooms, a kitchen, living room, and its own bathroom.

Back downstairs Bert took me through two sliding doors connected to the large living room. We managed to slip past R.G. who was still immersed in his ball game and newspaper. Bert told me the whole story about how this room was now a bedroom for my grandparents, but it was really supposed to be the dining room. I could tell because the built-in china cabinet was now full of linens. My grandparents had to use this room, she explained, because R.G. had lost a leg in a train accident and couldn't climb stairs.

In fact, that leg was the reason they were able to buy the house. Even though I was already afraid of R.G., this news made me want to run out into the living room to check him out again. I had noticed his glaring deformity, and now Bert explained why he wore a wooden leg which he kept propped up on the ottoman. According to Bert, R.G. used to work for the railroad. One day he tripped and fell when he was trying to run across the tracks to beat a train, and he ended up losing his leg. Ultimately, he was awarded a large insurance settlement and it provided enough money to buy and furnish this house.

I was aghast with the story, but Bert didn't skip a beat on her informative tour. After she pointed out the telephones in the downstairs living room and bedroom, she took me back into the entry hall. At the far end, past the staircase, was a swinging door which led into the kitchen.

"You must be hungry," Grandmere speculated as Bert and I pushed through the entry. She kindly offered me a small lunch.

I had been taken from the Williams' home just after one in the afternoon, and it was now around two-thirty. In the middle of the kitchen was a large wooden table and chair set where I sat to eat. I found it difficult to politely finish the meal because I was so upset and felt sick to my stomach.

In the kitchen I noticed a wooden hutch for the dishes and silverware, a Maytag refrigerator, and a big black-and-white stove. There were three windows, and in between two of them was the sink. The floor was linoleum, and there was a door, which led to a porch and the back yard. There was also a garage and alley at the back of the property.

In the middle of a conversation between Bert and Grandmere, a tall, well-built teenage boy bolted into the room. This was my seventeen year-old Uncle Charles. "He's a football and track star at the high school!" Bert proudly announced. He also had kind eyes, and they clearly captivated everyone's attention. I was overwhelmed by his presence.

Aunt Ruthie sauntered in only minutes behind him. She was fifteen and in the tenth grade. Her felt poodle skirt swished as she walked, and I couldn't help noticing her heavy, swirled bobby-socks. She plopped her pile of books down on the table next to me and said confidently, "Hi, kid!" She already knew me because she had come to visit me with Dorothy and Bert.

Now I was one of the girls, but the thought didn't soften the shock of the day. If I had been raised in a miserable foster home environment, I might have been thrilled to finally join my flesh-and-blood family. This wasn't the case. The Williams were my family and these people were still strangers. Only two hours had passed since I had been totally and unexpectedly uprooted.

How the rest of the day passed, and how I survived my transition to the new school, is hard to recall. I simply had to do it; there was no other choice. I wanted the Williams to come to my rescue, but I knew it couldn't happen. I rarely saw Dorothy or had anything to do with her during the first few days in my new environment, but soon I would find myself entangled with her in the battle of my life.

Chapter 4

Battle Lines

Only a few weeks after moving, I received my first beating from Dorothy. My foster parents had only spanked me once, but they cried with me and apologized for having to reprimand me. Thanks to Dorothy, I quickly learned the cruel difference between a spanking given in love and a brutal beating. It happened because I called her by her name, Dorothy.

"What did you just call me, you little yellow witch?" she shrieked. "I told you to call me Mommy, and I meant it!"

I stood defiantly.

"Now go and get R.G.'s belt and meet me in your room!"

I promptly marched down to my grandparents' bedroom to get the necessary belt, but I had no idea what to expect. As I dutifully delivered my mode of punishment to Dorothy's waiting hands, a totally separate person within my mind began talking to me!

"Don't worry, Jakii. We won't cry and we won't run or flinch no matter how hard she hits us," the voice told me. What followed is permanently seared in my memory. It was as though I was standing outside of myself watching it all take place.

"Take this, you witch . . . and this . . . and this," Dorothy repeated each time the belt slashed across my back, shoulders, arms, buttocks, or any place else the belt landed.

Why couldn't she call me by my name? I wondered as the force of the leather blows cut through my clothes. Somehow I was able to watch the event as an observer and I actually felt no pain.

I remember staring out the window as I received the blows, and at the very same time I was also standing beside myself observing the entire traumatic incident. I don't know how I managed it, but I honestly didn't cry or move. Later I named my "other" Jakii Miss Hyde, and "she" was the one who ended up dealing with all of my painful situations.

My composure so frustrated Dorothy that she threw the belt at me and ran down the hall. A few seconds later I heard her calling to the lady next door. They spoke through an open hallway window which was across from the bathroom.

"I'm beating her as hard as I can and she refuses to cry!" she yelled to Gladys. The neighbor must have told her to go back and beat me some more because she stormed back into my room and started the process all over again. She continued to beat me until she wore herself out.

"You're a stubborn, yellow witch," she pronounced in a huff before she finally gave up and left my room. I was grateful to Miss Hyde for empowering me, and somehow I was able to cut myself off completely from the physical pain. The battle lines had been drawn and war was declared. I had no idea why this woman, who claimed she was my mother, was always so angry with me.

The answer came many years later. I found out that Grandmere was the one who had worked so hard to get me into her home. Her oldest child, Dorothy, had delivered me at a girls' home for unwed mothers in Roseville, New Jersey, when she was only fourteen years old. It was a total disgrace to the family back in the 1940s to have a daughter pregnant out of wedlock, and even more of a disgrace for Dorothy to be so young. Dorothy claimed she had been raped, but in all fairness to her, this could have been her first boyfriend. Later she confided to me that she loved women, but often used men for money.

Dorothy had no name for me when I was born, and had no intention of keeping me. My grandmother wanted me to be part of the family, but it was the State Board of Health that determined the home they lived in at that time was not a healthy place for a newborn to live. It supposedly had something to do with the cellar. Therefore, I was one of the first black babies in the state of Pennsylvania to be placed in a foster home. My photo even made the local newspaper.

The main headline read: "Foster Homes Campaign Launched For Over Three Hundred Children." A subtitle claimed: "Seventy-Three Colored Need Homes." My baby picture went with the story and they described me as "a little bit of girl with bright dark eyes and a wistful expression that somehow brought tears at your heart." As the story read, my mommy had been too sick to care for me even though she loved me deeply! This obviously had been a story designed for the sake of the press rather than reality.

This foster care program in Pittsburgh had been launched under the sponsorship of The Federation of Social Agencies and The Community Fund. The last paragraph of the write-up made a plea. "Little Jackie wants a home . . . so do all the other seventy-odd youngsters. Parents who have taken such children into their homes to bring them up with their own babies, find no trouble at all. Wouldn't YOU like to be a foster parent?" The Williams' family stood in the gap for me.

By the time I joined Dorothy as a five-year-old, my grandparents had moved from the condemned house into the big house on South Euclid. In order to get me back into the family, Grandmere Alma went through the courts. She even arranged for Dorothy to marry the man she claimed had raped her. Grandmere desperately wanted her first grandchild to have a legal father.

Dorothy was nineteen when she married Cleophas Wright, my father, but they only stayed together a total of six days. It was hard for me to think of him as my real father because he moved out of our big house almost as quickly as he moved in. I hardly remember him even being there.

On the other hand, I always felt a special kinship with Grandmere. She was a beautiful lady both inside and out. According to Bert, she was educated and had worked in a bank before she married R.G. When I moved in, she was a silk presser at a local dry cleaners and had to tend to her own children, including myself. As if she didn't have enough to do, she also had to care for R.G. and protect all of us from him.

In a way, R.G. was the only man left to fulfill the father role in my life, but that never happened. As far as I could tell, R.G. loved three things: himself, his sister Elizabeth, and a fifth of Johnnie Walker Red. When I met him he was probably around forty years old and he wasn't exactly into healthy living. He was an excellent baker, and after his accident he worked for a bakery whenever he felt up to it. I remember R.G. best as a short and stocky man who loved his Italian stogie cigars and drank too much. His disposition was as bad as the smell of his cigars that permeated the house, especially while he was drinking.

The verbal abuse R.G. dealt out to everyone in the household kept me in a state of shock. In fact, I can't remember him ever being kind or friendly, but he often managed to beat each and every one of us, including Grandmere. But one day Grandmere flipped him on his behind and he never hit her again! He wasn't a worthy role model in any respect and I promptly learned to stay out of his way.

Even though my mother, Dorothy, was nineteen when she came for me, she was not the least bit interested in taking care of a child. She would be gone for weeks, if not months at a time, and when I did see her she was either ambivalent or resentful towards me. Things were actually better for me when she wasn't around.

On weekdays Dorothy worked long hours cleaning public buildings, but she was best known as the barker at a local strip club. It seemed odd that she liked to dress like a man, but she was always neat and clean and appeared to carry it off well. I remember watching her dance to jazz and rhythm and blues music when she was home. She and her older brother along with a few of her friends would sometimes discuss the new music releases.

I remember one night in particular when she was dancing to Dinah Washington and Billie Holiday music playing on the Philco record player in the living room. I peeked around the corner to watch, and she unexpectedly grabbed my hand and pulled me into the room.

"I'm going to teach you the swing," she insisted. I tried as hard as I could to follow her fancy moves, but she wasn't satisfied with the quality of my efforts.

"Bounce, you witch, bounce!" she demanded impatiently. "You're just like your father—you got no rhythm!" Humiliated, I managed to pull loose from her grip at my first opportunity.

It didn't take long to figure out that Dorothy had only two things on her mind: partying and women. Both men and women seemed to like her, but she became especially close to certain married women.

A woman named Dora boarded in the bedroom next to ours, and she had a daughter named Annie who sometimes played with me. I couldn't understand why Dorothy slept in the room with them, but I do know there was a lot of friction between my grandparents because they slept in our house together. Dorothy and Dora frequented the bars together and sometimes stayed out all night. On one occasion it was fortunate that Dorothy didn't accompany her, because that night Dora never made it home. We found out later that someone had poisoned her drink and she died. Annie had to move out and Dorothy was distraught for a long time.

After that, Dorothy returned to her other female friends and I wouldn't see her for weeks at a time. Grandmere worked during the day, so she couldn't take the full responsibility of caring for me. When Dorothy finally would come home, Grandmere would ask about the money she was supposed to be providing for me. She always had some kind of excuse and never paid up.

One time when Dorothy came home after being away for a month or so, she announced that she was pregnant again. All I could think of was the fact that we would have another mouth to feed and another kid to take care of. What a joy!

I remember the warm June evening when I saw my mother sitting on the front porch moving slowly back and forth in the glider. She was in her fifth month of pregnancy and I was almost eight years old. A sudden urge came over me. There was something I needed to know. I slid next to her on the glider and laid my head on her arm. We sat there for a moment or two, not saying a word.

The movement of the glider ceased. "I love you," I said softly ~~to Dorothy as I laid my head upon her arm~~.

There was no response.

"Do you love me?" I asked her.

"Get your head off me," Dorothy spat as she shoved me away from her. "Heck, no, I don't love you. I've never loved you!"

I couldn't believe what I was hearing. "I would have never brought you home from the hospital if it hadn't been for Grandmere," Dorothy continued. "Now get your butt away from me!" She ground out her cigarette in the ashtray which was balanced on the arm of the glider.

Her words took my breath away. It was as though someone had punched me in my stomach and I could not catch my breath for a moment. I don't remember how, but I got up and moved far enough away from her to stay out of her reach. I realized Miss Hyde was once again standing nearby on the porch, watching me stare at Dorothy in disbelief.

I had never felt so alone in the world. Miss Hyde posed the difficult questions: "How are we going to survive? Who is going to love us?" I simply didn't know.

Once I remember Mother Williams paying me a visit. It was very awkward and my heart yearned for her. Why didn't she see my pain and arrange it so I could go back to her house where I belonged? She talked to me and bought me an ice-cream cone, but I never saw her again. Why didn't she ever come to see me again? I always had more questions than answers.

Chapter 5

The Truth About Dorothy

I never seemed to acclimate to my new surroundings and life at 200 South Euclid Avenue didn't get any easier. The quest for my mother's love was a hopeless cause, and the birth of my brother Reggie only complicated the matter. I couldn't understand it, but Dorothy actually seemed to be fond of the little creature, and in no uncertain terms she continued to let me know where I stood with her.

Despite her show of favoritism to Reggie, she only stayed with him during the first two weeks of his life and her recuperation. Once her strength was back, she wasted no time getting back into her old lifestyle, and she rarely stopped by to even check on us. Just who did she think was going to take care of her new baby? As an eight-year-old I certainly didn't know the first thing about caring for an infant, much less having full responsibility for him.

It's true that Grandmere did what she could to care for him, but she also had to work. When I arrived home from school my shift began. It didn't matter if I had homework to do, because everyone else was busy. So it was either Grandmere or myself who had fed, diapered and comforted Reggie throughout the night. It sure put a dent in my ability to focus and concentrate at school!

However, Reggie was my little brother and I dutifully tended to his every need. My weekends were spent scrubbing diapers and clothes in an old-fashioned washtub using a galvanized number six board and Fells Naptha Soap. Modern conveniences were available, but by this time the gas and electricity had been turned off because Grandmere couldn't pay all the bills by herself and R.G. was not much of a contributor. Somehow I endured the humiliation of being poor, but one of the hardest burdens for me to bear was the fact that almost everyone in town seemed to know more about my mother than I did.

On occasions when Grandmere would make Dorothy take care of us, Reggie and I found ourselves living all over Pittsburgh. She would be living with whatever woman she was interested in at the time, and whether we were welcome or not, we were added to the mix. Thanks to Mom and Dad Williams, I knew a family was supposed to have a mommy and daddy. I thought it was odd not to have a father in the house, and it was even stranger having two mother figures who slept in the same bed without daddy there.

It also seemed peculiar that my mother preferred living with married women whose husbands were always absent for various reasons. Of course, at this age the subject of sex didn't even register with me. I was simply aware of the fact that the lifestyle I had to live was different from most of the kids at school, and there was something about Dorothy that other people looked down upon.

Dorothy would go to any length to please her special women friends and they often had more control over what Reggie and I did than Dorothy herself. For instance, one woman always had us go with her whenever she visited her husband in jail. Normally we would not have been exposed to such experiences, but whatever Dorothy's friends did with their own families, we ended up tagging along. Unfortunately, all of Dorothy's women cared more for their own children than they did for Reggie and me, so we were always the outcasts.

Perhaps the worst part of living with strange families was that Dorothy would often shower the other children with gifts in order to win the favor of her special friends. Of course, this was torture for us; it was agonizing to see these other children receive the very attention we craved.

The first time I had a clue that Dorothy was being more than a friend to these women was that terrifying night in Carrie's flat. As a twelve-year-old I had been afraid to open my eyes to see what was happening, but that unsettling incident made Dorothy and her women even more revolting to me.

As an adult, now I realize that I had heard these sounds before, but I always thought I was just having a bad dream. I could easily shake off the memory when I awoke the next day. At other times, I would be in another room and would barely be bothered by the noises because I would roll over and fall back into a sound sleep. However, the incident at Carrie's flat was different because I was there in the same bed with them. Their strange moaning sounds were loud and clear and the bed was shaking from their movements.

More than a year after that ordeal, I finally discovered the truth about what Dorothy was really doing with all her women. It was inevitable that one day I would come face-to-face with the truth, and when it happened it was another bombshell going off inside my very being. Once again, the truth was revealed in Carrie's flat. Even though Dorothy also stayed with other women, her relationship with Carrie spanned quite a few years. The events of that fated evening are still seared in my brain.

I had just turned thirteen and Dorothy had asked me to entertain a young girl named Heather who was visiting Carrie's neighbor. The "in thing" for young people to do at that time was to meet friends from school at Westray's Skating Rink for teens. I took Heather with me that night, but she quickly began whining that the guys wouldn't skate with her. Instead of trying to help her out, I couldn't wait to call it an early evening and get back to Carrie's building to get rid of her!

So, much sooner than expected, I was free of Heather and was climbing the stairs to Carrie's second-floor flat. Thankfully, Dorothy had given me the key so that I wouldn't have to sit on the hallway steps to wait for her and Carrie to come home from the clubs. I was told that another neighbor was taking care of Reggie, so I figured I'd have some time to myself. That was rare!

I slipped the key in the lock and heard the tumblers turn. With a twist of the knob, the lock yielded and I entered the room. As I moved my hand towards the light switch, suddenly I stopped my action in midair. I listened carefully as my eyes began adjusting to the dark. There were those noises again— the same ones I'd been hearing every time we stayed with Carrie. My eyes boldly moved in the direction of the source of the sounds, and the light from the window illuminated the scene quite clearly. In that split second I stopped breathing.

In the bed, my mother and Carrie were naked and hugging one another. Their moans and noises seemed to match their movements.

I stood dumbfounded! My eyes quickly averted to the foot of

the bed. Just as I suspected, there was Reggie in his usual spot. I prayed that he really was sleeping even as anger welled up within me like liquid fire. Once again I felt overwhelming fear flood my system.

I had never even imagined two women doing things like that to each other's bodies! Not wanting to be seen, I quietly pivoted, tip-toed through the door and locked it without a sound. I fled the building in a dreamlike trance and there's no doubt I was in a state of shock!

Who can we turn to? raced through my mind as Miss Hyde and I ran down the endless sidewalks of the city. Burning tears were searing my cheeks as I tried my best to erase the mental picture that was playing over and over in my mind.

So, that was what had been going on that night when the movement of the bed and the strange noises had awakened me! How could Dorothy and Carrie do such a frightful thing, knowing that Reggie and I were in the same bed—let alone the same room? *How could they do such a thing at all?* my mind screamed. Maybe this was what had been happening every night when I thought I heard sounds.

When I stopped running, I found myself standing in front of a Catholic church. On occasion Dorothy had made me attend a Catholic church, even though Grandmere also took me to her Baptist church with the rest of the family. Now, more than anything else, I needed comfort and insight. I entered the sanctuary through the double brass doors and saw a priest at the far end by the altar. I made my way down the long rows of pews to reach him and I realized I was trembling uncontrollably.

"Child, what's wrong?" he inquired as he took my hand. The only light in the huge empty church came from hundreds of flickering candles.

"I'm so mad at my mother," I began. "I just saw her doing

something horrible!" My words blurred together as I breathlessly recounted the entire scene detail by detail. When I finished, I searched his eyes for compassion and direction.

The priest stood for a while looking at me with disbelief. His advice then came quickly and stung my ears. "Now child," he began sternly, "You must ask God for forgiveness for being angry with your mother."

This time Miss Hyde spoke up because I was afraid to express my true feelings. "Forgiveness? I'm the one who is supposed to ask for forgiveness?" was the question I screamed back at him. Miss Hyde and I just didn't understand. "What about what I saw my mother do?"

Obviously, the priest never expected me to ask any questions. In condescending tones he continued, "I'm sure it isn't as bad as you think." He patted me on the head. "You need to ask forgiveness for your sins, and then you need to pray the stations of the cross. Now, don't forget to seek help from the Virgin Mary." Miss Hyde wanted to slap him as she watched and listened in grief.

No sooner had the priest said it than he was gone. I felt deserted and betrayed! I re-directed a battery of questions upward. *By the way, Lord, why can Dorothy get away with doing all these bad things to me and Reggie? What about what she's doing to these women? Shouldn't she be the one asking for forgiveness?*

There was no answer. If this was God's response to me, I wanted nothing to do with churches at all! It would be years before I would trust a preacher or priest again, and God sure wasn't showing Himself to be all that comforting, either! I felt abandoned and betrayed by everyone who had any say over my life at that point.

Suddenly, my entire body was limp as a rag. I was physically and emotionally exhausted. I certainly didn't want to go back to

Carrie's flat, so Miss Hyde suggested I go to Grandmere's house instead. No one was home at 200 South Euclid, but staying alone in that big eight-bedroom house with no heat or electricity was a more desirable option than facing Dorothy and Carrie. I would save that dreaded task for the next morning.

When I awoke the next day, I came to my senses. I realized there was nothing for me to do but to go back and face my life, with all its depravity, with Dorothy. My feelings of disdain and hate for Dorothy's choices never wavered and finally I knew what everyone else had known all along. Something was very wrong with Dorothy's relationships with other women, but I still didn't know exactly what it was or how to explain it.

Dorothy's next female partner was a lady known as Edna who also had a daughter. Dorothy supposedly married this lady, and although their live-in time together came in spurts, their relationship lasted over four years.

Reggie and I visited Edna's home several times for picnics and holidays, but I don't think her parents approved of their daughter's relationship with Dorothy. Later I discovered the letter of divorce Dorothy had written to Edna dissolving their marital arrangement. As a result, Edna entered the military, and her daughter was adopted by the grandparents.

Dorothy went on to give birth to two more children that I know about, and she ended up selling both of them! It seems that she was a surrogate mother before the world even understood the definition, and she realized there was money to be made in the process.

The first little girl was born when my brother was about two-and-a-half years old. I don't remember much about her except that she was born in West Penn Hospital. Dorothy carried her ten months and there was grave concern about her health because she was so overdue. I don't remember Dorothy bringing the baby home from the hospital, because the adopting family took her right away.

The other child, another girl, was born when my brother was four or five years old. She was born in the same hospital, but this time Dorothy did stay with her for a while. Instead of coming home to 200 South Euclid, however, Dorothy moved in with a friend who lived down the street and claimed she would keep the baby until the new parents paid her in full. Personally, I was relieved I didn't have to care for the baby myself! Still, Reggie and I would stop by to visit our little sister every day on our way home from school. After the baby was gone, we didn't see Dorothy again for several weeks. Not many things could keep her away from her choice of lifestyle.

As a barker at the strip club, Dorothy continued to find many women who would engage in one-night stands with her. It didn't seem to matter to her if she carried on with married or single women. Once I heard that Dorothy had to jump out of a second-story bedroom window when a woman's husband came home early and caught them together in bed. As the story was told, he actually pulled out a shotgun and threatened to shoot Dorothy.

For several years, Dorothy worked during the day as a cleaning person in the local tuberculosis hospital. She introduced Reggie and me to several women who had been patients, and we found out later that she was also "involved" with them even though most of these women were married. The more I learned about Dorothy, I came to realize that she was notorious in her day!

We never knew the names of most of the women she sought out because many of her relationships lasted only a few weeks. Still, there would always be a steady stream of women who complicated our lives. Not knowing where we were going to be from day to day created many predicaments that were difficult to resolve. For instance, if Reggie and I had to stay with one of Dorothy's special friends who lived on the other side of Pittsburgh, we had to take the streetcar or walk miles to get to school. Life with Dorothy was never easy!

When Dorothy lived with a woman named Teresa, their happy little family included Teresa the wife, Dorothy her partner, Teresa's two children and Dorothy's bonus daughter and son. Teresa was the one who took Reggie and me into the prison to visit her husband, and often I wondered what he thought when we all visited him. I hated going to that building, and I was scared out of my socks every time the guards locked the doors behind us. I observed Dorothy talking to him on occasion and I wondered if he knew that she was sleeping with his wife.

Teresa lived in a tolerable neighborhood, but after taking the streetcar home from school with Reggie, we had to climb up the long, steep stairs from the street to the project building. In the winter it was always dark and scary getting to her apartment. These steps were dangerously overgrown with shrubs and bushes.

The daughter of one of Teresa's neighbors was murdered under those steps one night, and it took the police several days to find her body even though the steps were in constant use. My mother never thought twice about the perils Reggie and I faced when going to and from school, even though many of the residents kept their children home or escorted them after that incident. Looking after us did not fit into Dorothy's plans, so we had to continue traveling as if nothing had happened.

At least Teresa's home had heat and there was usually food to eat. Dorothy would cook once in a while, clean the apartment, and even worked every day to take care of her new family.

It was amazing to me that she managed to do all of this for Teresa and never gave a thought to poor Grandmere who continually had to scrape together dollars to care for Reggie and me.

At Teresa's apartment, Reggie would have to sleep in the room with her children, and I was left to sleep on the couch. At this age, I always slept on someone's couch or floor unless we were at Grandmere's. Another uncomfortable aspect of living with Teresa was that Dorothy would use me as the butt of her jokes.

"Come over here, witch, and dance," she would command. Another hurtful request was, "Show them your report card, witch!" Her favorite phrase seemed to be, "If you don't hurry up, I'll knock the stuffing out of you."

Thankfully, we only had to stay with Teresa and Dorothy long enough for Grandmere to cool her temper. Rightfully, Grandmere would send us to stay with them because Dorothy had ignored us or continually refused to pay for our upkeep. Then Teresa would tire of having two more brats around, and the next thing we knew, we would be on the streetcar going back to the house at 200 Euclid Avenue.

Chapter 6

Those In-Between Times

B ack at Grandmere's home we faced different obstacles. There was rarely any food, no electricity, and all water for bathing or washing had to be heated on the coal burning stove in the kitchen. Thankfully, my grandmother had the foresight to have purchased a stove with a gas line on one side and a wood-burning range with metal plates on the other side.

Every morning one of us had to gather some form of paper, crunch it up, and place it inside the belly of the stove. Wood chips or dry twigs were added next, and finally coal and then charcoal topped off the fuel. A dab of kerosene oil and a match ignited the fire, and we on the way to heating water for bathing or washing dishes, cooking our food or ironing our clothes.

Grandmere and R.G. were the only working members of the family at this time. Her money would go to house payments and the purchase of food and coal. I loved Grandmere so much because she never stopped trying to make things better for us. She helped with the housework when she was home, but she couldn't help me tend to Reggie during the night because she had to get up early every morning to go to work.

My granddad worked on and off as a baker, but managed to spend all of his money on himself. He could have been hired back at the railroad, but he chose to spend his time nursing his leg and drinking Johnny Walker Red. Once in a while he would bring home a cake or pie for the family, but he never contributed any money for the actual care of the family.

My Uncle Ray and Aunt Bert tried to help me as much as they could with Reggie, but we were never able to go places or do anything outside of the home unless we took him with us. Unfortunately, Reggie was always sickly, and Grandmere would have to phone all over town to try and locate Dorothy to let her know that he needed to go to the hospital. Without Dorothy's cooperation, my life was laborious and oppressive.

On Sundays the kids would be getting ready to go to church and R.G. would be trying to keep Grandmere home by picking a fight or fussing about one of the older girls going to a dance without his permission. It would always end in someone getting beaten with his razor strap; sometimes it was the three of us, Ray, Bert, and myself.

Still, when I look back on those Sundays I can't help but laugh because they were like a three-ring circus. One Sunday morning after the usual "love-pats" from good old Granddad, my Uncle Ray came up with a plan to get even with R.G. They were to go into effect when the next Sunday beatings came around. When R.G. was asking which one of us wanted to be first, I was to say, "Me!" Step two involved my participation, as well. When R.G. was slinging the strap, I was to fall down on the floor behind him.

The next part of the plan involved me accidentally bumping into Granddad while he was trying to beat someone else. Ray had instructed Bert to lean on R.G. when he was swinging at her, and the strategy was that he would stumble or fall over because of his bad leg. By then R.G. would supposedly abort his attempts because he would know that we weren't afraid of him anymore.

Everything began as planned. However, the only drawbacks were that Uncle Ray did all the planning and none of the follow-through. Later he denied all knowledge of what had happened, and Bert and I were the ones who ended up catching the wrath of R.G. Oh, the joys of Sunday mornings!

The 200 block of South Euclid Avenue was a very mixed community. Those neighbors alongside us who faced the street got along by never bothering each other. They were a combination of Jews, Italians, and Gypsies. The neighborhood behind our house was quite different. Our back yard faced smaller wood-framed residences and flats that housed lots of black families. You might say that it was a mini-black oasis.

When I met with my friends in our large, communal back yard, I was in heaven. I'm sure we had our disagreements, but we never fought. Some kids liked to tease me, claiming that my braids were thicker than my legs and it was no secret that I was thin for my age. I was also teased because my skin was fair rather than rich brown, but I remembered that Mother Williams had told me not to worry about it.

I was well known for never wanting to do anything in the usual manner, but I always excelled at everything I tried. All the kids played baseball in the alley every Saturday, and sometimes we assembled for a game after church on Sundays. We also picked berries, apples, and plums every week during the season. Then there were basement dances—or socials, as they were called—at least twice a month.

Because Reggie and I often went without meals and considered a candy bar to be a feast, we learned the fine art of visiting our friends at their homes right at the supper hour. We counted on the fact that most likely we would be invited to eat with them. Later in the evenings, all the kids in the neighborhood would play a game of hoofer or hide-and-seek. In the summertime, the adults would sit out on their porches playing cards or just talking, so we were sometimes allowed to play as late as eleven at night. Wow, we thought we were really living like grown-ups!

My close friends were Libby, who always shared my hopes and dreams, and Catherine who lived next door. I never held it against Catherine that her mother was the one who gave my mother advice about the beating I received when I was five years old and refused to cry during my lashing. I also promised Catherine that I would never reveal her nickname to anyone in my entire life. To this day, I've kept that secret!

We all had crushes on Sammy and Earl, two of the cutest boys in our neighborhood. All the girls my age would pray that they would show up at our socials, and the older girls were after my uncles. Ugh! In my judgement, they really had no taste in guys!

When Earl's family moved, we were left with Sammy as our one true love. We thought he was the only boy in the whole world. I knew that I wanted to have a husband some day even if Dorothy preferred to live with women. In fact, I had long since determined that I would never be like my mother in any way.

Meanwhile, the condition inside our house slowly deteriorated. Not only were we without heat and food, but large gaps widened in the walls that sometimes resembled the size and shapes of different countries on our school maps. Reggie claims that I taught him to identify the outlines of different states by pointing to the cracks and holes in our walls!

The most difficult part of not having electricity, besides the usual hardships it caused on a minute-by-minute basis, was the fact that I had to walk down the street to the gas station to buy the fifty cents' worth of kerosene oil used to light the lamps. Of course, I had to march past Sammy's house each time, and he and other schoolmates often watched me carrying out this lowly deed which implied poverty. I was humiliated but I learned to do it with my head up!

When I was eleven years old, a new girl named Jackie moved into the neighborhood. She and her family rented the third floor in a house only four doors down the street. It took time, but eventually we became friends. It helped that we both shared the same name and the same boyfriend, Sammy.

One day she invited me to spend the night at her house. This would be a new experience for me and I was really excited. Grandmere agreed, so the event was on. After dinner we played in her room until it was time for bed, and once we were tucked in, Jackie and I began our secret talk. We imagined marrying Sammy, figured out what our houses would look like, and even determined how many children each of us would have. The thought that both of us could never be married to Sammy at the same time didn't ruin our fantasy.

We kept our conversation low, but we giggled when we talked about how cute he was. Suddenly the bedroom door flew open. "Just what are you doing to my daughter?" Jackie's mother demanded. She ripped the covers back and looked at me as though I had done something very bad. "Now, get yourself home!" she announced firmly with no further explanation.

That episode put an abrupt end to any overnight invitations I might have received from Jackie or any other friend in the future. I wasn't sure what it was that I had done wrong, and I was clueless to think that Jackie's mother might have projected my mother's lifestyle upon me. Whatever the problem really was, I made it a point never to share my hopes and dreams with girlfriends or anyone else again.

School was somewhat of a diversion from my confusion and suffering. When I was younger, I had wonderful teachers who nurtured my passion for reading and writing, and two of them incorporated principles from the Bible into the lessons. As each school year ended and summer vacation began, all the kids were excited about attending Vacation Bible School at a big church in downtown Pittsburgh. I was especially fond of making hand puppets to act out scenes from the life of Jesus.

I enjoyed learning who Jesus was and what He had done for me. If what they said about Him was true, then He was even with me that frightful night when my faith was deeply shaken by the priest. That damage would take years to overcome, but good seeds were planted by these Bible School teachers and these seeds were sometimes watered.

I loved going to Vacation Bible School because I could color, play with my friends, and eat a lot of ice cream. Years later I would come to find out that this all took place at the home church of the famous faith healer, Kathryn Kuhlman. I had to laugh because as a child I found myself sleeping through many of her messages.

Even though I enjoyed grade school, I wasn't allowed to participate in any activities because most of them required money to join or a signature from my mother. Forging Dorothy's signature was not a problem and I had been perfecting that skill for years. She also refused to write notes allowing me to return to class when I had to stay home to care for Reggie.

I knew that ultimately the school would send a truant officer to the house and I would be expelled if I accumulated too many unexcused absences, so I always wrote and signed my own excuse slips. Report cards presented similar problems because Dorothy would rarely be with me during the time period that parents were allowed to review them. Guess who ended up signing mine?

One grand day I participated in a school play and was out of my mind with excitement. It gave me that rare opportunity to become someone other than myself, and I felt admiration and respect radiate from the classmates who usually made a habit of scorning me. I had finally found my niche! However, true to form, Dorothy managed to squelch my interest in acting by telling me I was making a fool of myself. I was devastated.

Next, I wanted to study the violin in school, but Dorothy said she wouldn't allow that "darn noise" in her house. Finally, I asked if I could study the piano, and she laughed and told me to get those "white" ideas out of my head. She couldn't even use the excuse that we had no money because at my school the lessons were offered free of charge.

It was nothing short of a miracle when finally I graduated from Friendship Elementary School. Not only did I go through the pomp and circumstance for such an event, but I also received all kinds of honors and was chosen to be the class speaker! As I prepared to go to the big event, I was crushed because Dorothy announced she was not going to attend the ceremony and not one word of praise or happiness for me passed through her lips.

There was, however, one hope I had for my special day. I remembered that Dorothy had made an agreement with my father that she would pay for my dress if he would buy my shoes. I kept my fingers crossed every day building up to the big event. I didn't want to do anything to mess up my good fortune. I was actually going to get a new dress!

The night before graduation, Dorothy jumped into bed with Reggie and me. When she was home for short periods of time, usually she slept with us in the double bed. The smoke from her funny cigarette filled the air before she turned the lights out. All day long she smoked either cigarettes or pot, and the cloud of smoke just followed her around. Immediately she fell asleep, but I stayed awake for hours contemplating the excitement of picking out a new outfit the next day.

The following morning Dorothy woke up, lit a cigarette, and blew the smoke at me as I greeted her with a cheery hello. She knew exactly what was on my mind. After a long drag on her cigarette, suddenly her attitude and story changed.

"You witch, I'm not going to buy you a dress today or any other day!" she declared abruptly. Then she got out of bed and walked down the hall to the bathroom.

I chased after her in a daze. "But you promised to buy my dress! What am I going to do?" I cried hysterically. Miss Hyde wanted to know what "we" were going to do.

Dorothy just glared at me through her cloud of smoke. "You're lucky I'm letting you go, you witch!" was all she had to say on the subject.

I was mortified! Frantically I woke up Aunt Ruthie, who was home on leave from the Air Force, and reported what Dorothy had said to me. She thought about it and came up with an idea. "Don't worry, Jakii. I'll talk to her and then we'll find your father."

I never found out what Dorothy told her, but by nine-thirty that morning we were on our way to find my father. I had my doubts because I knew Daddy didn't have that kind of money. My father was an alcoholic and barely hung on to any of his jobs. He was often known to paint houses while he was drunk.

Aunt Ruthie and I finally found Cleophas, thoroughly drunk, and clinging to the top of a ladder as he painted the third story of a house. What a sight he was! When I got his attention and explained the problem, he firmly insisted that he had no extra money for my dress and could do nothing about it. Fortunately, his father and uncle were working with him and somehow forced him to cough up the money for my dress, stockings and shoes!

With my newly-acquired fifty dollars, Aunt Ruthie and I ended up shopping for my first dressy outfit. The one we found was beyond my expectations, and Ruthie even combed and styled my hair as my crowning glory for the event. I was allowed to wear earrings and a little lipstick, and despite the deep hurts, I was a princess again at least for a day.

But joy always seemed short-lived when Dorothy was around. Shortly after graduation, I began to stand up against my mother's abuse. I can still clearly remember one evening in particular, when Dorothy and I got into an argument over a favor that I had done for my Aunt Roberta.

I still liked to call her Bert, but at this point my youngest aunt had grown up, gotten married, and even had a baby. Her husband was in the Air Force and Bert had been waiting all day to find out about a "hop" he had set up for her that evening. She had waited as long as she could for his call, but finally she had to go to the bank to cash a check for her trip.

While she was gone, her husband called our neighbor with the information. The woman asked me to come over to her house and get the message for Bert, but I knew I would have to pay for my kind deed since Dorothy had ordered me not to leave the front porch. I was only gone about ten minutes, but when I came back and encountered Dorothy on the staircase in the main hall, she gave me a powerful slap across my face without even asking why I had left the porch.

"You witch, get upstairs because I'm going to whip your butt for disobeying me."

I remained on the step above Dorothy, as I tried to explain why I had left the porch. "Bert needed that information," I yelled. "And if you ever attempt to hit me again, I'll kill you!" Miss Hyde managed to come through loud and clear.

Dorothy must have believed me because, from that day on, she simply stuck to calling me names, swearing at me, putting me down emotionally, and asking me who I thought I was. She made sure to keep me informed that I was a nobody and no one wanted or needed me, but she did keep her distance.

That same year brought about changes in my body that I didn't really understand. My period began briefly when I was twelve years old. I remember it started on Easter Sunday and lasted only two days. Little did I know it wouldn't show up again for an entire year, but I was deeply concerned and confused. Dorothy had never explained what would happen to my body at that age, so I had to draw my own conclusions.

The inside scoop from my girlfriends was frightening. If you kissed a boy, you would get pregnant! My friend Libby and I had both kissed one of the neighborhood boys, so one Saturday morning before the ball game in the alley, I told her my problem. In hushed tones I shared with her, "I must be pregnant because I kissed Joe and now I've stopped having my period!"

Libby was really concerned. She had also kissed Joe and missed her period, too. Since we both knew we were going to be in trouble with our mothers when they found out that we were going to have a baby, we decided to be friends for life and support each other. Then we ran outside to play ball.

By the time I was in eighth grade, Reggie was starting kindergarten. This meant I had to take him home and stay with him after his half day was over. I was on the verge of being expelled, but one of my teachers, Mrs. Stars, decided to check into my problem. Her solution was to send a note to all my teachers asking them to give me all my assignments before lunch each day so I could complete my work at home. Thanks to her, the school office finally stopped keeping track of my absences and tardies.

That same year, when I was thirteen, my period started again. I hid my underwear because I was frightened about what was happening to me. I was sure that I had done something horribly wrong and I knew that when Dorothy found out about it, she would beat me. Hiding the panties was the only solution I could come up with.

It was Grandmere who discovered the evidence in the back of my closet and told Dorothy to talk to me and buy a box of pads. The next time she was home, Dorothy looked for me and said she wanted to meet me in the girls' upstairs bedroom. Her voice didn't sound any too happy.

"What the heck have you been doing?" she yelled as she held up a pair of the dirty underwear. "Who the heck you been messing with?"

What did that mean?

"And don't try to sit there and look so innocent!" she screamed with an accusatory glare.

I was truly frightened, so I just sat on the bed staring at her and tried to figure out what was going to happen to the baby. Miss Hyde wondered if Dorothy knew that "we" were having a baby because I had kissed a boy.

"I'll not even waste my time or money on a tramp like you, you little yellow witch!" Dorothy announced. "I'll give you all you're gonna need!" She pulled out a piece of a white sheet from a bureau drawer and ripped it into several wide strips. Throwing them at me, she concluded, "Use these, you witch! This is all you'll need anyway."

Dorothy got up from the bed, and without another word of explanation about what was happening to me, she turned on her heels and walked out of the room. I heard the front door slam as she left the house.

Tears rolled down my face. I couldn't understand why I always did something that made Dorothy furious with me. I was learning to look forward to the days, weeks and even months when she would not be around to cause me such grief.

Dutifully I wore the strips of sheets for the next few days until I broke out in such a rash that I could barely walk. Grandmere noticed how I was walking and asked me what was wrong. When I told her about the sheets, she put her hand under my chin, turned my face up toward hers, and looked into my eyes. "Tell me why you're walking like that and why you're wearing sheets between your legs."

I explained what Dorothy had instructed me to do. Grandmere immediately made me undress, and when she checked me over, she cried. She drew a bath for me and put some powdery stuff in the tub. She stirred it around with her hand and had me sit in the hot water for a while. It was very soothing, and when I finished she gave me one of her pads to use. I was to tell her when I needed another one.

I had only seen my grandmother extremely upset once or twice before, but she lit into Dorothy as soon as she came home that following week. Thankfully, my mother never made me use sheets again, and eventually I learned enough to realize that kissing could not get a girl pregnant! That was the best news I had heard to date.

Today it seems strange to me that, although I had witnessed Dorothy in bed with Carrie, I still did not associate their behavior with sex. The full comprehension of this term alluded me for years, but at least now that I was in junior high, I was ready to take on a more mature relationship with the boys my own age.

Chapter 7

First Love / First Betrayal

His name was Johnny. He had blonde hair and deep blue eyes. His skin was the most beautiful golden tone I could imagine, and it looked great in contrast with his hair. Whenever he smiled at me I felt my world change.

His mother was white and his father was possibly half Indian and half white. Whatever mix he was, his father did not like blacks. Johnny lived in Mississippi most of the year, but his family came up to Pittsburgh to spend the summer and some holidays. They stayed with his older sister who lived down the street from me. I officially met Johnny my seventh-grade year, but he never noticed me. He was different because most of the boys who were older than me thought that I was too young to play with because of my slight figure.

When Sammy told me that Johnny was coming again to stay for the summer, I worked myself into a frenzy just thinking about seeing him again. When I thought of him I felt my heart race, but I pretended it didn't matter. It was probably a week after school let out when I finally caught a glimpse of Johnny. I was hiding in our living room and watching from behind the shade in hopes of seeing him. My wish came true—and even more!

Johnny walked up to my house and when he was almost at the front stairs, he turned and looked directly at the front window where I was hiding. I couldn't move. He was looking right at me. I was hoping he had not seen me, but I was captivated by his beautiful eyes and the tenderness of his smile.

Johnny must have caught me peeking because he stood for a moment, waved to me and then continued his walk. Now I couldn't breathe! I was elated, excited, ecstatic! This happened every day for at least a week until he finally motioned for me to come out of the house.

"What am I going to do?" The question resounded throughout my body. Somehow I gathered all of my courage and walked to our front porch and down to the landing of the second set of steps where he was standing. I held my breath.

"I've been looking for you," he said coolly. "Want to sit down and talk?"

I thought I must be going deaf because I just knew this couldn't be happening to me! He . . . Johnny . . . wanted me to sit and talk with him? I couldn't speak. I could only nod my head and smile.

He quickly put me at ease and we talked for hours. He told me about his parents, his home in Mississippi, and how much his mother was against him talking to me.

"Why?" I had to ask. "You've never really talked with me before now."

He went on to explain that last summer he had told his mother and sister he had met the most beautiful girl and that he wanted to marry her. I wanted to faint.

When his family had arrived in Pittsburgh a week or so ago, he showed his mother the house where I lived. We lived on the same block, but my house was at the beginning of the street and they stayed at the other end. His mother informed him that a "colored" family lived there and he was not supposed to have anything to do with me. He yelled at his mother, announced that he could like whomever he wanted and ran out of the house.

After our first talk, he became a light in my life and I saw him every day. I freaked out when Dorothy decided she wanted to take Reggie and me away with her to some woman's house to stay for a while. I was so nasty about it that she sent me back home in a hurry and I ended up having the greatest summer.

When I had to go to the store, Johnny would walk with me. After my chores were done, he would come and sit on my steps and we would talk endlessly. Sometimes he would hold my hand. Oh, how my heart pounded with excitement! When all the kids played hide-and-seek, we would stick together. It was during one of those hiding games that he first put his arm around me. My heart seemed to actually stop beating! Never in my whole life had anyone, except Mrs. Williams, been so sweet and loving to me. Even when Dorothy cut my hair off, he told me I was pretty.

The other guys were beginning to complain about Johnny spending so much time with me, and the girls began their teasing. We played baseball with the gang every Saturday, went to some of the basement parties, but I arranged it so I wouldn't have to kiss him when we played spin the bottle. Even when I had a chance to choose him, I didn't because I was afraid to let anyone else see how much I cared for him. This always ended up hurting his feelings, but it was hard for me to find the words to explain why I didn't want others to know.

As Johnny walked me home one night he asked if he could kiss me. How could I resist? I can still feel his kiss to this day. He held me close and told me over and over that he wanted to marry me. Nothing would ever change his mind, he proclaimed. He said he would wait for me because he was sure we were supposed to be together. I could tell it came from his heart and I honestly believed him. Johnny was sure that nothing—not even his daddy's prejudice nor the time we would have to wait for each other—could keep us apart. Of course, he had never met good ol' Dorothy!

When Johnny went home at the end of the summer, he gave me a compact with a mirror, a promise to write, and a picture we took at the arcade in the Woolworth Department Store. He did write to me and sent a picture, and he wanted one of me as well. In the meantime, Dorothy got wind of him and wanted to know the details. I told her how much he liked me and explained that the feelings were mutual.

Dorothy glared at me as she delivered her edict. "You'd better keep your mind on those school books, you witch, and not on some white boy! You should know by now that all they want is sex!"

Exactly what was sex? I still didn't really have a clue. Even though I had seen Dorothy naked with another woman, I didn't associate their actions with whatever men and women did to make babies. My friends always talked about having babies after they got married, but none of us were quite sure how that happened.

Dorothy carried on about my boyfriend all year and told her friends that for some reason I thought I was better than everyone else because I wanted a white boy. I tried to ignore her, but I didn't understand why Johnny kept asking me when I was going to write back to him in his letters. I wrote to him constantly, so I realized that for some reason he wasn't getting any of my mail! I asked his sister, who lived nearby, to send a letter to him for me, and the mystery was solved. We figured out that I never received all of his letters, and very few of mine even made it to the post office. Dorothy was trying to undermine us!

Still, in his letters he continued to plan for our future together. He was sure it would only take four years for us to get married, and he tried to figure out how we could see each other more often. His efforts weren't in vain. By the time the next summer rolled around, he had talked his parents into allowing him to permanently live with his sister in Pittsburgh. I was on cloud nine!

I couldn't wait for the summer vacation to begin. I desperately wanted Johnny to go with me to my last school picnic hosted by Friendship Elementary. They were always held at Kennywood Park, and the school gave us free tickets and the school buses picked us up and took us home for free.

My grandmother and our neighbors always packed some serious lunches, and no ride in any theme park could match the "Whip" and the "Jack Rabbit." Dorothy promised me that I could go and she was actually going to stay home to watch my little brother. She had no idea that Johnny would be there.

When Johnny arrived in town he found me at school and walked me home. Even though I was out of my mind with joy to see him, I was also terrified someone would see us and tell Dorothy we were together again. I knew that one mistake could cost me the school picnic.

As we walked, Johnny proudly announced that he didn't care who saw us together or what anyone said. I felt just like the princess my foster father always called me. Johnny came to my house that evening and we sat outside and talked. He kissed me and we danced to the music my Aunt Roberta was playing on the record player inside. We were never really able to be alone because my aunts and uncles were always somewhere close by.

The day before the picnic, I explained to Johnny that I would not be able to see him because I had work to do in order to be free to go to the picnic with him on Saturday. He said he understood, but he still came by at least four times just to say hello, to bring me lunch, or to just sit and talk for awhile.

My friend Libby knew how excited and happy I was and she kept watch for Dorothy. Johnny said he wasn't afraid of Dorothy and that he didn't think she was so bad. How odd for him to say that since he had never met her. If he only knew! Still, it was better that he didn't know her because he might have heard some of the things she had to say about me. I would have been crushed!

All that day I scrubbed, cleaned, washed, dried, folded, and ironed for all of us. I made Dorothy's bed and changed her sheets, and just so she wouldn't have to cook anything for Reggie the next day, I prepared the food. I carefully thought it through and tried to do everything she could have possibly asked me to do.

As I got ready for bed that night I was deliriously happy. I attempted to hug Dorothy goodnight, but she pushed me away as usual. Still, I thanked her again for letting me go to the picnic.

She grunted, "You just better behave yourself or I'll kick the stuffing out of you!" That sounded just like Dorothy! I promised to be perfect, and she added one more thing for me to do. "Just make sure you wake me up in the morning before you leave."

As I was getting ready about nine-thirty the next morning, Johnny knocked at the front door. The first bus was going to leave at ten-fifteen, and most of the kids wanted to be on the first two buses because fewer parents would be there. When I started to walk to the door, I heard Dorothy ask me who was ringing the bell.

"Oh, it's just one of the kids I'm riding out to Kennywood with!" was the safest reply I could think of in short notice.

"You tell them you're not ready yet and they'd better come back later!" she instructed.

As I opened the door, I felt that usual twist in my stomach which usually signaled that Dorothy was about to go into one of her crazy spells. I hoped beyond hope that Dorothy didn't suspect anything.

"I can't believe you're not ready yet!" Johnny exclaimed.

I dropped my head and lowered my voice as I tried to quickly fill him in on my situation. "My mother said I can't leave until she gets up. Maybe I can catch the next bus," I suggested in exasperation.

Johnny was okay about it and kissed me on the cheek before he left. He also said that he'd return for me.

When I made it back up the stairs, Dorothy was full of questions. "Was that the white boy from down the street?"

I couldn't lie, so I admitted the truth. I softened it by explaining that Johnny, Poochie, Sammy, Libby and her sister Janet were all planning on riding out together.

"You just go feed your brother! You know you can't leave before I'm ready to get up," she growled. At least she didn't throw a fit that Johnny had been there. I dressed and fed Reggie and finished getting ready myself. Johnny came back to the door again, but Dorothy still would not allow me to leave. The third time he returned, Johnny was upset and Dorothy was just being mean.

"If you don't get rid of that white boy, I will!" she screamed. I was pretty sure I knew exactly what she meant. I tried to explain to Johnny that my mother had decided not to let me go and that I was very sorry. His perception was that I was just making excuses because I did not really want to go with him. He looked so hurt and wanted to know what he had done to upset me. All I could say was that he had done nothing wrong and I was having a typical Dorothy problem. He finally gave up, and his parting words were that he was still going to the picnic and he hoped to see me there later.

I closed the door in tears. I had wanted to be like all the other girls at the picnic who had boys with them. I had dreamed of having him hold my hand, sitting next to him on the roller coaster ride, and floating through the "Tunnel of Love" while we kissed. I wanted everyone to see us because I had never been popular. All the kids knew about Dorothy and how she lived her life. She never tried to hide anything, so none of the other guys ever wanted to date me.

Even though some of the adults may have partied with Dorothy and her women friends, they certainly didn't want their daughters to befriend me and their sons were not allowed to get close to me, either. Johnny had been the only exception. He had heard all the rumors about Dorothy and even saw her go out with his sister's neighbor lady. However, he told me that his dad drank too much and beat his mother, so everyone had something to be ashamed of. I thought that was one of the nicest things he could have said to me.

Now my special day was being ruined because of Dorothy's bad attitude toward me. She managed to stay in bed all morning, and then around two in the afternoon she decided to finally get up and visit a friend who lived behind us. This woman was the mother of one of my neighborhood friends, Poochie. While Dorothy was there, Poochie's mom must have reminded her that she had promised to let me go to the picnic. When Dorothy came back to our house, her attitude had shifted dramatically.

"You can go now, witch, but you can only go with Poochie. You'd better not hang out with that red-neck white boy or I'll curse him and his family out!" Dorothy intently stared into my eyes and wanted to know if I was clear on her rules.

At that point I didn't care. My only thought was to see Johnny again so I could explain what really happened. Poochie had promised to tell Johnny the truth, as well. The moment we arrived at the park, I spotted Johnny near the gate. All day he had been hanging around the entrance waiting to see me as soon as I arrived.

When Johnny saw that my escort was Poochie, he turned red in the face and accused me of standing him up. What about all the promises we had made? This was my burning question as my heart started to shatter. Johnny was crying and Poochie could not get a straight word out of his mouth because he had a problem with stuttering. The situation broke my heart. Johnny and I both ended up crying, and Poochie kept trying hard to get out the story about my mother. Poochie was under pressure because he knew what Dorothy said she would do to Johnny if I didn't get rid of him.

Finally Johnny walked away, thoroughly convinced that I had chosen another boy over him. Every time I saw him that night, he was on one of the rides with another girl. I went home early and cried all night. Why did Johnny refuse to believe me when I tried to explain things? It didn't make any sense to me! In fact, it still brings tears to my eyes when I think of the look of pain on his face that night.

Days or weeks later, I'm not even sure because it seemed like a hundred years, I saw Johnny again. I was coming home from the store and he was walking toward me. He wrapped his hand around my upper arm and just stood very close to me for a minute before speaking. In quivering tones, he told me that just before the picnic someone informed him that Poochie and I had been seeing each other during the school year and we were a serious couple.

I was dumbfounded! He went on to say he did not believe the news until he saw Poochie and me walking to the park gate together that afternoon. He assumed that I had led him on, thinking that I wanted to go with him when I was really planning to go with Poochie all along. He said he would have preferred hearing the bad news from me.

I tried to explain to him that the story he heard had no truth to it, whatsoever!

He came back with a stinging question. "Why would your mother lie to my sister about that if it wasn't true?"

My whole world exploded. Dorothy had betrayed me!

Why had she planted the lie? She knew that Poochie and all the kids I played with were just friends. Besides, when she asked me if I liked Johnny, I didn't lie. How could she be so cruel? What had I ever done to her?

Johnny continued, "I'm sorry about what you had to go through with your mom, but you shouldn't be a liar, too!"

"What?" I screamed in disbelief.

"All you had to do, Jakii, was tell me the truth about your new boyfriend. I never want to see you again." He paused with great emotion. "Now I hope I can forget you as quickly as you've forgotten me!"

Nothing I could say would change his mind, but I could never forget him. I constantly carried the guilt of the way he was treated for years. Years later, at age 43, I decided to write God a letter about Johnny and tell Him all about what happened that summer. I asked for God's forgiveness, and prayed He would allow Johnny to forgive me for the hurt he went through. Ever since that summer, I've always wanted the opportunity to try one more time to tell him the real story and how I've never forgotten him!

The rest of summer vacation that year was a painful blur, but changes were in the air. I was bracing myself for my first year at Peabody High School and despite my heartache, I could only hope that in high school my life would change for the better.

Chapter 8

Those Cold Winds of Change

St. Claire Street, Pittsburgh, Pennsylvania. . . 1958 – 1960

Entering high school brought many new challenges, but one issue always remained the same. My brother and I had to survive no matter where we laid our heads to sleep. Grandmere's house had always been our temporary home base, but by this time, problems were beginning to develop there as well.

Sometimes Grandmere didn't remember who we were or where she was. By this time she was in her late forties, and the doctors blamed her bad memory on high blood pressure. My aunts told me she had suffered from it all her life, and the doctors claimed it had begun to destroy her brain functions.

"That's why," they tried to explain to me, "she doesn't remember you sometimes." You can imagine the sick sensations of fear and insecurity I felt when the most stable person in my young life began fading away! Neither Reggie nor I could possibly understand the depths of what was happening to our special Grandmere. Finally, the doctors discovered the real problem: Alzheimer's disease! Being home at 200 South Euclid Avenue was never the same after that painful revelation.

In fact, it wasn't long before everyone had to move out of the big old house and our world turned upside down. Our house had been taken over by the state for back taxes, so each of the family members had to find their own places to live. Grandmere was the first to go and went to live with my Uncle Raymond and his family because she was so sick.

Uncle Raymond had always been the most fun-loving and the warmest of all Grandmere's children. He was the tallest of the boys, was great at football and track, and he was musically inclined. In high school he had been in a singing group which performed at parties and he enjoyed tap-dancing. Both Uncle Ray and Uncle Charles were offered athletic scholarships to college, but neither of them decided to go. Instead, Uncle Raymond got a job, married a woman named Barbara (whom I adored), and together they had three sons.

My grandfather, R.G., had already left South Euclid two or three years before Grandmere was forced out by the city. His excuse was that his sister Elizabeth was sick and needed him. *Well, what about my grandmother?* I wondered. R.G. moved in with Elizabeth and never returned home, and to my knowledge, no one missed him. My impression of Elizabeth was that she was a mean, dried-up old woman who was eaten up with jealousy over my attractive and gracious grandmother!

Aunt Ruth, or "Ruthie" as I called her, went into the Air Force as soon as she graduated from high school. She traveled a lot during her tour of duty and surprised us all when she came home pregnant. There was no husband in sight, and after my cousin Ashley was born, Ruthie modeled herself after Dorothy by developing a preference for women.

I thought it was admirable that Ruthie tried to save the old house by applying for a loan through her job. My grandfather agreed to sign a quick-claim deed over to her so that she could get the loan and pay off the back taxes on the property. This would have kept the property in the family and when the city of Pittsburgh came through with renovations, they would have had to pay my grandparents for all that land they redeveloped in the area.

However, R.G.'s sister, Elizabeth, talked him out of signing the deed over to Ruthie by telling him that his daughter only wanted to steal the house away from him. Of course this wasn't true. The loan was only for three thousand dollars they owed in back taxes on the property. The bottom line was that R.G. listened to Elizabeth, the city took the property, and R.G., Ruthie and Elizabeth never received anything.

Dorothy was the oldest of all the children and Uncle Charles was only two years behind her. Dorothy had established the family tradition of getting pregnant out of wedlock and Uncle Charles followed suit by getting his girlfriend pregnant. Grandmere saw to it that both of them married, and even though Dorothy wiggled out of her marriage to Cleophas, Charles married and stayed with his wife, Lily. He was a fairly quiet and methodical man and ended up being a very good father to his children. To his credit, he remained very loyal to Lily until his death in 1991.

Uncle Charles and Aunt Lily had lived with us on South Euclid, rent free, as long as they could. Lily made an immediate impression on all of us by putting a lock on "her cabinet" in the kitchen so that no one would eat her food. Even Grandmere wasn't allowed to touch her stash.

Roberta and I just couldn't resist causing havoc by breaking open her conspicuous locks, raiding her cabinet, and then blaming the deed on R.G. Lily knew that we were guilty, but she couldn't prove it. Eventually she stopped locking the silly cabinet, and no one ever bothered her things again.

The youngest of Grandmere's five children was my Aunt Roberta. She was two years younger than Ray and five years older than me. If it weren't for her care, I could have never made the transition into this new family. Bert took me in as her instant best friend, and that relationship never changed through the years. Bert had always been my role model, and I wanted to grow up and be like her.

By far, Bert had the best figure of all the girls, and she was a master at hair and makeup. Her skin was a smooth bronze color and her smile was like her mom's—it could light up any room! To top it off, Bert was so talented that she was offered an art scholarship when she was thirteen or fourteen years of age. Then, at sixteen, she became pregnant and married Ralph. He was in the Air Force and they were stationed in Texas for awhile. Absolutely no one was happier than I when they moved back to Pittsburgh several years later.

We all said our good-byes to the once stately old house on 200 South Euclid Avenue, and from this point on, Reggie and I were left solely to Dorothy's mercy. When she finally ran out of people to unload us on, she ended up renting a third-floor flat for us on St. Claire Street. Like most of the other houses on the street, it was an unimposing brown frame house with a nice porch on the front.

To get to our rooms, we climbed the stairs to the second floor, walked to the end of the hallway, and then unlocked the door which led to the third floor. Once inside the door, we had to walk up another flight of stairs, down the hallway, and into each room in our flat. The address just happened to be about three blocks away from the house where Dorothy had stayed with her fourth child. We didn't know if it was a curse or a blessing, but Reggie and I basically lived there alone.

Later we found out that Dorothy was able to pay for the flat because of an accident Reggie had been in when he was three or four years old. My little brother had been hit by a car while riding his bike and he ended up going through surgery to have a pin placed in his leg. Dorothy received a settlement for his injuries, and the money was supposedly placed in trust for him until he turned twenty-one. Thanks to Dorothy, Reggie wasn't told about the money until he was 18 years of age and by that time, I don't think there was even a hundred dollars left out of the five or six thousand dollar settlement he had been awarded.

Our new third-floor flat was at least adequate and the rooms were large. On the other hand, the rooms were much too dark in spite of having windows in every room. The hallway led to a moderate-sized living room, a bedroom, kitchen and a bathroom. It was nothing fancy, simply adequate. There was a tiny balcony off the living room, but we had to keep the doors locked because it was too unstable for us to stand on.

The kitchen was depressing because we rarely had any food, but the cabinets were stocked full of roaches. We stayed out of that area most of the time. We did have the use of Dorothy's radio and record player because she wanted to be able to enjoy her music whenever she stopped by. Of course, that didn't happen very often.

It was my responsibility to make sure my brother ate, slept, went to school, and stayed out of trouble. It was fine with me because I loved Reggie and felt an overwhelming need to protect him, but sometimes I wondered who I was protecting him from. Not many situations could have been worse than being deserted by your own mother. Then again, I guess we could have been on the street!

On a warm summer day in July when I was 15 years old, Dorothy put Reggie and me on a streetcar to visit Bert and her family for a weekend. When October rolled around, we were still there! Once the school year started, every weekday we traveled back and forth between East Liberty, where our schools were located, and our aunt's house in Homewood.

The driving time between the two parts of town was about thirty minutes, but the walk took almost two hours, depending on the depth of the snow. We would start our trek as early as 6:45 in the morning and we made it back to Bert's around five in the early evening. Our walk was often done in the dark of early morning, or during dusk and nightfall in the winter months. The journey would have been even longer if we had taken time to avoid the bars, and the alcoholics who frequented them. But we were used to seeing it all, so we walked through the area without giving them or the bars a second thought.

On occasions when we did stay in the flat, Dorothy would drop by once a month to leave us a few quarters. With the grand sum of fifty cents I would buy fresh hamburger meat for fifteen cents, a large can of pork and beans for fifteen cents, a loaf of bread for a dime and finally a nickel package of Kool Aid. Sometimes the neighbors would loan us some sugar. We tried to make this precious food last for three or four days, but for the rest of the month we became scavengers.

Once again we tried to visit friends during the supper hour, and sometimes we made our way to Uncle Charles' or Uncle Ray's house. Unfortunately, Uncle Charles' wife, Lily, didn't like me very much because of my antics from the past and she would only feed Reggie. Our only other option was for Dorothy to take us to Carrie's house to eat, but that didn't happen very often anymore. (We didn't mind because Carrie was not too hot of a cook.) If there was any food at all in the house, I had been taught to always feed Reggie first, but many times we both went to bed hungry.

Whenever Dorothy stayed overnight with us, we knew something was out of order in her life. Possibly she was between lovers, she was sick, her lover's husband was home, or maybe she just remembered she had two children. I'd like to believe she sometimes remembered us.

One afternoon when Reggie and I were sitting on the front porch of our house, we watched a man with a little girl walking toward us on the street. I took note because I thought I recognized the child. Her face reminded me of my brother's features when he had been much younger. Suddenly it clicked in my mind. There was Reggie's littlest sister and my half-sister who was just shy of two years old. I guessed her father was taking her to see Dorothy's friend who had cared for both mother and child before the baby was legally adopted.

I stared at the little girl as she toddled down the sidewalk. She was laughing and obviously proud of herself for her newfound ability to get around. What a wonder it was to watch her! Her little arms flung out to her sides to help her balance, and she looked so happy. Her "daddy" was just beaming until he suddenly looked up and noticed Reggie and me observing them from our front steps.

I had met this man when Dorothy was in the hospital. Later, he and his wife had come by the house of Dorothy's friend when they were there to make final arrangements for obtaining the baby. As soon as he saw me, I was sure he remembered me, too. His immediate response was to pick up the child, turn around and quickly walk back up the street. I wasn't sure why he didn't want Reggie and me to be around them, but that was the last time either of us ever saw her. Reggie didn't really understand the significance of the situation.

The only real drawback to our flat was that it only had one bedroom. Dorothy awarded it to Reggie, and even though it was furnished with two twin beds, I was not allowed to sleep in his room. Dorothy bought an old sofa with a built-in hide-a-bed for the living room and this was to serve as my bed. On those rare occasions when Dorothy did spend the night with us, she joined me. Ugh—I hated that! But to this day, I cannot tell you why I felt that way.

I recall her foot touching me one night while I was trying to sleep, and I drew back my leg and kicked her with all my might. She didn't show that she was aware of what I did, but she never accidentally touched me again when we slept together. I learned to get into the bed first so I could fall asleep before she joined me.

Another one of my tactics was to wait on the steps leading up to the living room until I knew she was actually asleep. Then, I would get into bed and lay on my side so I couldn't see her. I also made sure I held the bed frame tightly so I would stay far away from her reach.

The sofa bed caused me trouble even when Dorothy wasn't around. The mattress was full of bed bugs! I soon discovered they were famous for biting and drawing blood. Their bites would leave sores that scabbed over when they healed. The mattress also housed fleas because a cat had slept on it before Dorothy purchased it.

I was quite a treat for the fleas because if one flea was within a thousand miles of me, it would bring the whole family and they would have a feast at my expense. The bites itched, and naturally I scratched. I had more scars and dark spots on my legs and arms than I could count, and they ended up causing me more embarrassment in high school than any insecure girl would ever want!

As a sophomore I decided to try out for the majorette squad. It was the least I could do since Dorothy would never allow me to take the piano lessons I longed for. I also was shut out of social circles because of Dorothy's reputation, so I decided this was something I could accomplish on my own. I ended up being the second black girl ever to make the majorette team. For another one of those rare moments in my life, I was on cloud nine again!

However, the victory didn't come without obstacles; I needed money for the boots and the baton. Dorothy just about had a stroke! Still, I stood up to her and refused to back down. She never seemed to be moved by my desperate pleas, but sometimes when my situation was pitiful, Dorothy's siblings chipped in for me. In this case, one of my uncles gave me the money for the boots.

The day Bert took me to purchase my marching boots was rather pathetic, but hilarious as well. I put one on, stood up, walked to the mirror and then burst into laughter. There was my skinny leg coming out of what seemed like a huge white leather boat. Bert and I laughed until we were almost sick.

Bert tried to soothe it over by telling me that I didn't look that bad. Finally she convinced me that my legs would fill out soon, and in the meantime I should just wear two or three pairs of socks when I marched. Again, Bert was right!

As for the rest of the uniform, my father bought the baton, Bert gave me her white blouse, and the rest of the uniform, including the skirt and sash, was provided by the school.

I could never thank my aunts and uncles enough for helping out when Dorothy let me down, but still I faced another obstacle, to pass my peer review. The open sores and scars from the bedbugs and fleas still marred and covered my legs.

Fortunately, once again Dorothy sent Reggie and me out to Bert's place in Homewood for an overnighter which turned into another four-month stay. My aunt wasted no time coming up with a remedy for me. Every day before and after school, Bert would have me bathe my legs and arms in warm water with Epson salts and then apply a camphor salve after it was dry.

Within one month all the sores had healed, and by the day I marched for our first performance, you could not even find a scar. The socks worked to fill out my boots when I was marching, I didn't even care how skinny I looked—I felt great! I had one of those "princess" experiences again, and by now I really appreciated them.

I loved Bert! She continued to come through for me in so many ways. If she had not loaned me her clothes and shoes, I would have had to wear the few old clothes I had packed for that "overnight" stay for four months straight. Bert drove me to the flat on St. Claire Street to retrieve some of our clothes. We found the rest of Reggie's school outfits, but mine were nowhere to be found. Later Dorothy told me she had packed my things somewhere so they wouldn't get lost. Actually, there weren't enough items to lose! Another time she told me she threw them away.

Despite Bert's assistance, other experiences at Peabody High School brought me back down to where I lived. I ended up having to pay for quite a few extra textbooks because Dorothy delighted in putting her cigarettes out on their pages whenever she saw me reading. Of course, I had no money to pay for replacement books, so the librarian came up with a plan. She arranged it so I would work a few hours with her a couple of days a week in order to make up for the money I owed. To be honest, I never minded because I was able to become familiar with most of the books.

Reading had become a means of escaping the hurt and pain of my daily life, and I had even received an award for the most books read by a student in a single year. I was such a voracious reader that I would even walk to the store while reading a book. Every chance I could get, I immersed myself in biographies and stories about people who lived in faraway places. Some of the romance stories I read told of families with children who were loved by their parents, and the heroine always had a best friend, and eventually a boyfriend who asked her to marry him.

Therefore, my own fantasies were based on having a warm, loving mother and a father who thought I was their princess. When things became too tough with Dorothy, I would retreat into a book, or if she forbade me to read, I would write my own stories or create an imaginary room or house in my head that didn't exist in Pittsburgh. I always created a fantasy into which I could conveniently slip to hide until the storm around me was over. If things became too tough. Miss Hyde would appear and often go toe-to-toe with Dorothy until she backed down.

It never made sense to me that Dorothy could be so upset with my desire to read. When her friends were over, I would hear her telling them that I thought I was so much better than the rest of the family because I always had my head stuck in a book. "She thinks that's going to make her smarter! I'll still kick her butt and show her who's smarter!" she would brag.

Even without any effort on her part, my mother's reputation managed to follow me through my high school years. As expected, I was never invited to parties or sleep-overs at my classmates' homes, and once again, the kids knew more about my mother than I really understood. When I was fourteen, some students began making fun of me by telling me that my mother was a "bull-dagger."

The old saying, "Sticks and stones may break my bones, but

names will never hurt me," was certainly not true for me. I knew Dorothy dressed like a man and didn't even walk like other moms, but I had no idea what the term "bull-dagger" meant. In fact, all the expressions my classmates used to describe Dorothy haunted me.

Shortly afterward I heard the new term, I ran into my "Uncle" Bobby. He wasn't really an uncle, but was a close friend of my Uncle Charles. He stayed with our family for a while when we lived on South Euclid, but ended up living with us until he married or moved in with a lady. So we just started calling him "uncle." He might as well have been my uncle because he was part of the family, and I trusted him enough to ask him about the mysterious words I had heard.

"Why are you asking these questions?" he wanted to know.

I was ready to come to terms with the topic, so I didn't hesitate. "I once saw Dorothy and Carrie doing something to each other in bed, and I wonder if the term 'bull-dagger' has anything to do with it?" I bravely revealed.

"Jakii, that term refers to a woman who likes to keep company with women rather than men," he explained, then added his own thoughts to the definition. "Maybe they were born different." He went on to explain why people used slang terms like that. "It's similar to someone calling me a 'cracker,' a 'nigger,' or a 'greaser.'"

Because I had lived in a very diverse community for nine years, it wasn't hard for me to grasp his meaning. I also learned that day that the most common terms for Dorothy's kind were words like "queer" or "dyke." I thanked "Uncle" Bobby for his insight, but my next thought filled me with panic. I directed this question quietly toward God.

Lord, does that mean I have to be like Dorothy? The question had often crossed my mind, but this time I trembled with the idea. If

"Uncle" Bobby was right about his idea that Dorothy had been born that way, did that mean that I would turn out that way, too? This thought began to haunt me and in my mind I screamed, No, *no, no!* In the midst of my panic, another thought came to my mind. *I'd better ask a priest before I get myself in trouble questioning God and my mother!*

Despite my old wounds, I made a point of going to the Catholic church the next week. That's as far as I got. I never asked my questions because I could not find a good-looking priest to hear my confession. A few of my Catholic girlfriends and I had made a habit of going to church on Saturdays to look for a handsome young priest who would listen to our make-believe confessions. Our goal was simply to be in the confessional alone with the best-looking priest of the day! I'm ashamed to say the whole idea had nothing to do with our religious convictions.

Strangely enough, the way in which "Uncle" Bobby explained my mother's lifestyle also made me question if there was really anything wrong with her. *Maybe she's normal after all,* I tried to reason. I didn't know of any other females in our part of town or neighborhood who dressed like Dorothy or spent all their time with women, so I had no one with whom to compare her.

Even though the derogatory words my classmates used for my mother stung me, I had to try to find some joy in my life. Sometimes that happened in brief and unexpected moments. Remember the boy that every girl in grade school wanted to marry? Sammy! Well, in high school he finally kissed me!

He had always been a friend of mine even though his parents didn't want him to hang around with me. Still, we managed to visit and have talks. One day Sammy was having a casual conversation with me on my front steps, and he ended it with that long-awaited kiss. It was a one time thing, but what a thrill!

The downside of that cherished event was that my best friends, Catherine and Libby, had already moved away from the area with their families and they could not revel in the glorious moment with me.

Although Reggie and I sometimes had reprieves at Bert's house, we were basically living alone for two-and-a-half years at the flat on St. Claire Street. Most of the details involving our day-to-day life in that dark, solitary place still remain a dense fog in my mind. In general, I know that Reggie and I had to leave an hour early each morning, on an empty stomach, to make it to school, and when we came home I was overwhelmed with homework, majorette practice, preparing dinner or locating food, washing our clothes and cleaning the house.

Washing clothes was one of the biggest chores because I had to scrub them in the bathtub and then hang them to dry on the clothes line in the back yard. In winter, we just hung the various pieces up in the flat and hoped they would dry before we needed to wear them again, which was usually the next day. While I tended to all my duties, Reggie and I would listen to the radio, and then we finally went to bed.

Once in a long while when Dorothy did straggle in during the evening, I would be up half the night fetching for her or sleeping on the floor in my brother's room because she and her friends would be partying in the living room where I usually slept. For me to shut out the exact details of our lives, I know they must have been pretty bleak. Then again, I had no idea how much worse things could get.

Chapter 9

The Shadier Side of Life

I was finally understanding more about Dorothy's lifestyle, but that never made me feel any better about myself or made my life easier. No matter what she did, Dorothy ended up affecting my life in profound ways. Ninety percent of the time, I would have no idea what she was involved in until something bad would happen; usually I had to live through the events one at a time before I could look back and assess the damage.

During high school, I started noticing how she was branching out in her work in very disturbing ways. Aside from her regular job, or between lay-offs, she learned to give abortions. Again, I wasn't exactly clear on what it was all about, but she was in great demand! I remember once when Dorothy was home with us at the flat, she received one of these "business" calls.

"I've got to get my kit," I heard her say to the caller. "Now you realize, this time I'm going to get my money up front. Right?" When she hung up she actually told me she was going to someone's house to give them an abortion. She never bothered to hide a thing from us! The next thing we knew, she was gone.

Unfortunately, that wasn't her only new job. I found out she also cut, packaged and sold drugs, and I was often the person she would send to deliver the packages. Several times a week she would put me in a cab and would say something like, "Take this over to Betty's house, witch—and make sure you come straight back!" Although she would send me in a cab, I usually had to walk back home or catch the street car after the mission was accomplished.

I never knew much about drugs at that time, and I most assuredly didn't know what they did to the people who used them. The kids at school talked about sneaking a beer or smoking a cigarette, and the really bold ones smoked a little grass when they could steal it from their mom or dad. But the only people we knew who took drugs were the men who leaned against the poles or building scratching and nodding after shooting up on heroine. The common terms for drug-users then was what I was taught by my mother's crowd—"junkie."

There I was delivering drugs as if I was a dealer and did not have any idea what I had or what it was used for. If I had been caught and arrested during my deliveries, I would have been clueless of my crime. Somehow Dorothy always had a way of putting me at risk.

Ironically, it was my Aunt Roberta who finally told me about drugs when I was fourteen. She explained how bad they were and that I should never let any man or woman give me any. She claimed that if she ever heard of me taking drugs, she would personally kill me herself. She really made her point, but quite a few years later I found out that she let some junkie turn her on to heroin. She should have taken her own advice!

Dorothy, too, was hooked on heroin for a while. There were

two stories surrounding her addiction. One was that she was going with a woman who was strung out on heroin, or "horse," as she used to call it. The woman insisted that Dorothy try it because it was supposed to enhance their love-making. I don't know how much of an effect it had on their relationship because Dorothy got strung out very quickly. Their affair didn't even last long enough for her to introduce her new lover to any of her usual running buddies. I knew this because her friends were phoning my aunts and uncles asking what was wrong with Dorothy.

The truth was that Dorothy was dealing drugs for the mob. Everyone knew the mafia existed in Pittsburgh, but no one dared point out the members. Dorothy was obligated to give them the money she made from the sales and they were supposed to pay her a share of the profits. But, trying to be slick, she came up short. Either she spent the money, or she may have kept too much of the drug supply for herself. Whatever the situation, the price of error was going to be steep!

One morning I found her on the front steps of our flat. We didn't know it, but someone had shot her full of heroin and pushed her out of their car in front of our place. At the time, I had no idea why she was so sick and was throwing up all the time. I did the best I could to care for her for almost two weeks, and then she was off again without a word of explanation or thanks.

On another occasion, I finally made the connection between the drugs and the sickness that followed. Again Dorothy got strung out. This time she locked us up together in a sleazy hotel room somewhere in downtown Pittsburgh and instructed me in advance not to let her out of that room under any circumstances until the job was done. I was about 14 or 15 years old and I was not prepared for what I was about to see and experience.

She had to go through cold-turkey withdrawals, she explained, and I was to be there for her. It was horrible watching her scream and sweat, and at the same time she would claim she was freezing. Her body was visibly shaking. It was frightening!

The small room had a bathroom with a toilet and sink, but bathing was difficult because it smelled bad in that place. There was only one bed and a few blankets. I didn't know exactly where I was, and there was nothing for me to do or eat. Once a day a man or woman would come by the room and bring towels, a sandwich or soup and chocolate candy bars, and tell me to make sure she ate one. I must have stayed with Dorothy for four or five days and the walls of the room, as well as my stomach, felt like they were caving in on me. I tried to stay out of Dorothy's way until it was time to wash her up or help her to the toilet.

Dorothy threw up the first few candy bars, and at first refused the orange juice. I remember that I had to keep washing her things in that horrid tub because we both had only the clothes on our backs. When it was all over, Dorothy just said, "It's time to go." At least, to my knowledge, she never went back on heroin again.

How did I feel during that horrific experience? Once again, my mind automatically shut out the experience and the memories. All I can truly remember are the bare facts and the newfound knowledge that drugs were very dangerous. Also, my mother had used me again without affording me any thought or consideration. As a robot, I simply did what I had to do and life went on.

When I was fifteen, Dorothy informed me that I would be starting a wonderful job working at the same place where she and her friend Donna worked part time. The location was in a very affluent suburb of Pittsburgh at that time, but I wasn't clear on what the business was all about. According to Dorothy, my job would be to make the beds in a five or six bedroom home and I would be paid one hundred dollars a week.

I could have been delighted with such an easy job for such good money, but for some reason I didn't like the sound of it. Also, I knew better than to trust Dorothy and Donna. I remembered that my grandmother worked eight hours a day in a dry cleaners, and she only brought home one hundred dollars for a whole month's work. So why were these people going to pay me that much money a week just for making beds?

Not knowing what to do, I sought advice from my Aunt Barbara, Uncle Ray's wife. Aside from Bert, "Aunt Bar" was my favorite aunt because she always took extra time to explain things to me. I told Aunt Barbara about the job offer and asked what she thought. She frowned as she listened, and then agreed that something didn't seem right to her, either. She promised that before she confronted Dorothy or told my Uncle Ray, she would do some checking around.

Since Ruthie had returned from the Air Force with her daughter, she had turned to the gay lifestyle. Ironically, she was usually interested in the same women Dorothy was after. In this case, she was attracted to my mother's friend, Donna. So, Aunt Bar decided to approach Ruthie with the story about my job offer and ask her to find out what she could from Donna. Of course, Ruthie was more than willing to check things out.

As Ruthie later reported, the house where I was supposed to work was not a simple family dwelling. It was some kind of exclusive ladies' club full of women who were looking for young, new talent. It was my mother who had suggested me for the job. When Aunt Bar and Bert found out, there were some major sparks flying!

Now both Ruthie and Aunt Bar were furious with Dorothy. Ruthie was mad because she felt that Dorothy never treated me right, and she also knew that if she exposed the plan, it would drive a wedge between Dorothy and Donna. Of course, this was an ideal set up for Ruthie because that would mean Donna might end up being available to her.

Aunt Barbara was livid because she felt this was a horrible thing to do to a child, especially your own daughter. When they finally confronted Dorothy, the feathers flew! Dorothy denied the entire thing, then called Donna and threatened to do her bodily harm for telling "lies" about the job. Their relationship was definitely over. Immediately Donna sent a telegram to Dorothy stating that she was suing her for slander. Dorothy, in turn, said she would sue Donna for attempting to prostitute a minor. Nothing ever came of it, and I never had to take the job.

Later, I received the wrath of my mother concerning the entire episode. "If you'd kept your darn big mouth shut, you witch, you could have made good money and no one there would have touched you!"

"If the job was so good and legitimate, why didn't you simply take me and Aunt Bar or Ruthie out to the house to meet the people? That could have cleared up any misunderstanding," I retorted.

"You're just like your father!" Dorothy snapped back. "You can just kiss my butt! I have nothing to prove to you or those other nosy witches!"

As it turned out, Aunt Ruthie did win Donna's affections and they lived as a couple for nearly eighteen years. Together they raised Ruthie's daughter, my cousin Ashley. During the years that Ruthie and Donna lived together, no one from our entire family wanted anything to do with Donna. Finally, even Ruthie had enough of Donna and left her. No one could imagine how they lasted that long!

I was beginning to see a clear pattern of homosexuality that seemed to be passed on through our family. I learned that my great-uncle, my grandfather's brother, was also gay and very flashy about it. So I made a deal with myself that if I ever thought I was becoming like Dorothy, I would kill myself. With that heavy sentence, I was even more aware of the fear that one day I might wake up and find myself gay!

Now, with Dorothy's wrath heightened because of my refusal to take the job, the question was brought up again by Miss Hyde. "How are we going to be able to stay out of Dorothy's way?" There just had to be a means of deliverance!

Chapter 10

The Stand-Off

By the time I was sixteen, Dorothy sent me back to live at Bert's house in Homewood. The lights and gas had been cut off in our third-floor flat on St. Claire Street, and Reggie and I were literally freezing to death. Dorothy was living with Terri, another one of her lovers at that time, and she was not making payments on the flat or providing us with food. Finally I told a family member about our problems, and she must have gotten in touch with Dorothy and told her to send us to Bert's again.

The arrangement with Bert was that we were only going to stay with her family for a weekend but, as usual, that weekend turned into another extended stay. After about three months, Bert's husband, Ralph, phoned Dorothy to tell her she simply had to send money to help feed us. After all, he already had a wife and three children of his own. After Ralph left for work, Dorothy called and told me to get my brother and go back to the flat on St. Claire Street.

"Dorothy, are you crazy?" I asked. "You know we don't have any money for streetcar fare and it's dark and cold outside!" It was the day before Halloween. Also, I was having a lot of pain from my period and had been bleeding for over 30 days. I went on to tell Dorothy about my medical problem and took the opportunity to scold her, "The school nurse told me you should take me to see a doctor!"

My statements about the living conditions outside or inside of the St. Claire Street flat, and the mention of my physical problems, didn't seem to phase her. "If you and your brother don't get your butts home immediately, I'm going to come over to Bert's house and beat the stuffing out of you!" she threatened.

At this point I was incensed enough to take a stand. "I'm not going to drag my brother home to that dark and cold third-floor flat! The gas is shut off and it's too cold to stay there—and you know that!" I screamed at her. "You'll just have to come on over and beat me because I refuse to walk home!" Dorothy slammed the phone down, and within twenty-five minutes she pulled up in a cab.

Bert told me not to worry because she would not let Dorothy hit me and that she would attempt to reason with my mother. When Dorothy came storming in, Bert pulled her aside and tried to explain the female problems I was having. Bert told Dorothy that she and Ralph had attempted to get treatment for me, but since I was a minor and Bert was not my legal guardian, the doctors could do nothing.

None of this meant anything to Dorothy. She turned her rage on me and proceeded to call me every name under the sun. The venomous lecture that followed was about how hard she had slaved to give me everything I ever wanted.

How could this be? I wondered. Sometimes one of my aunts, or an uncle, would take pity on me and buy me a new blouse, skirt or shoes, but none of these necessary items ever came from Dorothy. I knew Miss Hyde had to have her say! "My shoes have holes and all my clothes are hand-me-downs from your lover's children or one of my aunts!" I shouted.

My courage was building into a fury and Miss Hyde again urged me on. "Don't you think I know about your friends? I know you have female lovers! And you have always cared more for one of them then you ever did for me or Reggie," I raged on. "I know exactly what your lifestyle is and you've never done a darned thing for me!"

I couldn't stop now. "All your money goes to support these lovers of yours, and their children, too! And the last time you ever bought me anything was a pair of socks for Easter four years ago. You paid for my brother's entire outfit, and bought Theresa's children some clothes, but you only invested in one pair of socks for me!" I kept blasting away. "And when you threw those socks at me, you know what you said. 'You witch, you better be glad I got this much for you!'"

I almost wanted her to strike out at me so I could fight back. For a while she just stared in disbelief, but she had a few more choice thoughts to deliver. "Don't you know how kind my women have been to you, you ungrateful witch?" she thundered. "They allowed you to sleep on their sofas and they have fed and clothed you!" Then she balled up her fists to swing at me. Her right fist was about to land in my stomach when Bert made a timely entrance back into the room.

She grabbed Dorothy's wrists and held them firmly. "Hey, sis! Don't you know the pain this kid is in? She's been passing blood for over a month now and you've refused to take her to a doctor!" Bert was thoroughly disgusted with her.

"You have two choices, Dot! You either get your affairs in order so there's heat in the flat, or take the kids to live wherever you're staying. And you'd better get some medical attention for Jakii, 'cause if you don't, I'll tell the family about it!"

Dorothy was irate. No one in the family ever went against Bert. Even though she was the smallest of the sisters, she had a reputation for not taking back talk from any of them. When Bert got mad, everyone knew to watch out, and even her brothers wouldn't go against her! So Dorothy wasn't about to attempt to fight her or hit me now that Bert had her say.

Instead, Dorothy again turned her verbal wrath on me. "You witch, what's on your back right now is all you'll ever get from me 'cause I'm giving away or burning all your junk. And, you will never set foot in my place again!"

I knew she meant it. With that parting speech, she abruptly turned and yanked Reggie by his arm, grabbed his coat with her other hand, and promptly exited Bert's house. I was a junior in high school and I never lived with her again. Thankfully, Bert found it in her heart to continue to house and feed me.

Several days later, Bert had to rush me to the emergency room because I was still bleeding. The staff held me there for hours while the police attempted to find Dorothy in order for her to sign the necessary papers which would allow the doctors to treat me. When they couldn't find her by four in the morning, they put the wheels in motion to obtain a court order to treat me because of my weakened condition and tremendous loss of blood.

Dorothy arrived just ahead of the court order, signed the papers and promptly left. She never even asked if I was dead or alive, nor did she stop in to speak to me. While I was in the hospital, she only came once because of a direct request by my doctor. He had to tell her of my condition and needed to get her permission to perform minor surgery.

My stay only lasted a couple of days, but my brain was in a fog. I can't remember if the nurses were friendly or curt, but basically I was alone—really alone because Dorothy had washed her hands of me and didn't seem to care if I lived or died. My mental dilemma overshadowed the surgery and my pain, and all I remember is that I came through it alive.

When I was released, I returned to Bert's house in Homewood, and I was truly grateful to her for watching out for me. However, now that I was a permanent part of her household, I found myself involved in a part of her world which would end up changing my life forever.

Chapter 11

The Rape of Innocence

East Liberty, a community in Pittsburgh, Pennsylvania. . .
1960 – 1962

Living with Bert helped put her past in perspective for me. During our long talks, Bert revealed she had been only seventeen years old when she married Ralph. I had been too young to be aware of it at the time, but her wedding came about as the result of a baby-sitting job she decided to take. One night Bert had been caring for children who lived next to the place where Ralph lived or was visiting. He saw her there, and before she knew it he was inside the house. As Bert told it, he raped her that night and she became pregnant.

Grandmere's idea was that a child should be with its proper mother and father, so she insisted they get married. Bert was beside herself, but Grandmere had her way. When they were first married, Ralph was in the Air Force and they lived in Texas, but later they moved back to Homewood, an area of Pittsburgh.

Together, they had three children.

Ralph used to beat Bert quite often when the family wasn't around, so she finally kicked him out. When I first started living with my aunt, Ralph was in and out, but Bert eventually made the decision to move to East Liberty in order to live alone with her children. Of course, I had to move with her. In her new location she dated other men from time to time, but her new steady was a man named Earl Brown.

When I was seventeen and a senior in high school, Bert decided to give Earl a birthday party at his place in Homewood. Naturally, I was there. During the party. Earl kept insisting he wanted to show me his new car. "It's just outside the house, sweetie," he pleaded.

Somehow, I just didn't feel right about it. "I'm going to have to ask Bert," I countered in order to stall.

"No, you don't have to do that!" he quickly explained. "I already told her I was going to show you the car." Earl grabbed my arm, pulled me out the front door and down the stairs to the street. There was his polished new car, but I was too nervous to be impressed.

"Get in and let me take you for a spin around the block," he insisted.

"I don't think I can do that," I told him firmly.

Still, Earl opened the door and pushed me into the front seat. He kept reassuring me that my aunt knew he was going to show me his car and she had said it was all right. "You know how many times she's sent you on errands with good ol' Earl," he reminded me. "What you think I'm gonna do to you anyway?" he quizzed in a derogatory tone and just would not stop. "After all, you and my cousin Dee are friends, and you're just like a sister to me."

Earl got in the driver's side, slammed his door and off we

sped. As it ended up, he didn't keep his word about a simple drive around the block. Now I was getting scared, but he kept talking about how great his car was performing. He wanted to know if I was enjoying the ride.

"I really think we should go back to the party because Bert's going to be angry!" I insisted.

With that, he pulled over into a vacant lot behind some homes and apartments. He turned off the car, grabbed me by my hair and forced my head back to kiss me. When my hand came up to block his advances, he grabbed my wrist and pulled my arm over behind my head. He let go of my hair as I turned to avoid the pain in my shoulder.

Earl had quite a hold on my left arm, as fear and adrenaline shot through my body, he quickly snatched my right hand and pulled it over my head, as well. With his body weight he pressed me down onto the seat, locking my hands down between the door and the side of the front seat.

It was by far the most vicious fight of my life. Earl tore my dress and underwear from my body, and without a defense in the world, he proceeded to rape me. I don't remember anything except extreme pain. I tried to hold my breath thinking that it could possibly be just a bad dream. No, it was an experience I could have never dreamed of up to this point. If this was what sex really involved, it was a horrible thing!

Sometimes I tried to scream, but he would either grab my throat, which cut off my air, or kiss me to keep me quiet. I don't know which was worse. My head was in such a position that I could look up out of the window and see all the windows in the homes around us. Some people were even looking out at us, but not one person bothered phoning the police for help.

During the ordeal, Earl kept knocking my right knee against the steering wheel, and that only added to my pain. When he finished, he pulled himself up, stepped back onto the ground outside his door, and then leaned over me so closely I could feel the heat of his breath on my face. "Do you love me?" was what he wanted to know!

I wanted to throw up! I opened my mouth to spit out my answer in his face, but I heard this strange voice coming from inside me whisper, "Yes." The voice was unrecognizable, and I have no clue as to why "yes" came out because that was not even on my mind. Maybe it was Miss Hyde trying to smooth over the pain and protect me, but she had never before backed down from anyone or any situation! I'll never know.

After I answered him, he supported himself over me by placing his weight on his left hand which was positioned on the seat next to me. He brought his right hand from behind his back, and it was then I heard a click and saw a flash of something shining. His breath burned my raw face as he pronounced, "If you'd said you didn't love me, I would have cut your throat and left you here!"

I froze without breathing, and with a smug look he put his knife away. He released my hands by opening the passenger door, and told me to put on my undergarments. Earl got back into the car and drove me home to Garfield Hill where Bert lived. Of course, he was full of instructions.

"If you tell anybody what happened here, I'll come back to get you. Besides, nobody's gonna believe you!" he predicted. His warning continued, "If you ever tell my cousin Dee, I'll come back and kill you."

When I walked through the front door, Bert was already home. "Where on earth were you?" she demanded.

Despite my fear, I didn't hesitate. I told her what Earl had done to me, and although my dress was torn and bloody and my hair was a mess, she continued to yell at me. "And just why didn't you phone me to let me know what was happening to you?"

I couldn't believe her harsh response! *Does she think there was a pay phone handy for me to escape the rape and call her for help?* With that thought, all I could do was cry and run down the hall to the bathroom to try and wash the filth of Earl off me.

My clothes and underwear were soiled and torn, and I still had blood trickling down my leg. When I got into the tub, Bert joined me in the bathroom. As she looked at my clothes, she began to cry. Bert told me to get out of the tub because she was going to take me to the police station. She had settled down and now was so sorry she had not believed me when I first came in. I think she was in shock. I knew I was!

At the police station, the examination was almost as bad as the rape itself. The accusatory questioning concerning the event was even more humiliating. The entire experience was nothing but another nightmare and I was sorry I had even subjected myself to the officers. They had to place my right knee in a splint to keep it immobile. Once I made it back to Bert's, I ended up staying in bed for almost two weeks, and my knee hurt so badly I could hardly walk with the help of crutches. There was no way I could return to school—I was so ashamed!

Two days after Bert and I filed charges, Earl sent two of his friends to our house to try and persuade me not to follow through with the case. They told me I would be damaging Earl's life if there was a trial. He had supposedly told them the whole story from his egotistical point of view, and his sidekicks thought I shouldn't punish him for what I had "asked him to do." They offered me money to drop the charges. Once again, I felt raped.

There I was, lying flat on my back in the bed. My leg was badly bruised and the kneecap had swollen to the size of a cantaloupe. My wrists and hands were black-and-blue from being forced down between the door and the seat, and the rest of my body was bruised. All I could do was cry.

Our family friend, "Uncle" Bobby, lived next door to Bert and had seen the guys come into the house. Thankfully, Bobby showed up at our front door and Earl's comrades made a hasty exit. "Uncle" Bobby then took me next door to stay with him and his wife, Evelyn, for a few days. He wanted to ensure that no more of Earl's friends would show up unannounced.

Amazingly, Dorothy did drop by and I begged her to sign me out of school. I only had four months until graduation, but I couldn't imagine facing everybody. I would be known as the town slut, and the disgrace would be even worse than the reputation I had suffered for years. Dorothy coldly refused and told me I could make it. According to her, I had to go back to school and face whatever was to come. It was a bit harsh, and perhaps she refused me out of spite, but for once Dorothy told me to do the right thing.

When I did return to high school, all the kids stared at me as if I was some sort of freak, and Earl's cousin, Dee, refused to speak to me. I stopped her one day in the hall between classes to ask her why she was being so rude.

"You lied about my cousin and I hate you!" she brazenly reported. "If he has to go to trial or jail because of you, I'm gonna kick your butt!"

For me, that was the final straw. Miss Hyde spoke up again to protect me. "You might as well start fighting me now because up to this moment I've been hesitant about going to court. Thank you, Dee—you've just made up my mind!"

I turned and limped away, and Dee never said another word to me again or ever tried to back up her threat. After graduation, I actually tried to get the charges dropped because of my concern for my brother, Reggie. He was still in elementary school and I was pretty sure he was not aware of Dorothy's lifestyle. I surely didn't want him to hear about the trial and all the mudslinging.

Earl would most likely bring up everything about Dorothy in his attempt to color me as a loose, immoral girl. After all, my mother was a lesbian and, in that time, that made me just as bad. I explained all of this to the District Attorney, but he told me I couldn't drop the charges because I had been a minor at the time of the offense. Earl was out on probation, and the police said they needed the trial in order to put him back in jail.

So much for trying to cover every base because the trial was a joke. Earl attempted to bring my mother's lifestyle into his testimony, but even his own attorney stopped him. I thought it was because my case was so strong, but I was dead wrong. In the end, Earl was only found guilty of committing adultery and the rape charge was dismissed. No punishment was due! It seems Earl was married at the time he committed the rape, and regardless of all the blood samples, my torn clothes, and the semen samples that were presented from the police examination, the jury took just thirty-five minutes to make their decision.

What had happened to me didn't seem to matter to the jury. It didn't phase them that I was a minor when I was raped, and the police even had the knife with Earl's fingerprints on it! Later I discovered the real problem. At that time, in the state of Pennsylvania, apparently a black person was never sentenced for raping another black, and so the all-white jury concluded that no crime had been committed.

I left the court alone feeling raped for the third time. Needless to say, Dorothy didn't even bother showing up at the trial. Only God knew what I had gone through! It's interesting that years later someone told me what became of Earl. A friend of mine had just run into him a few weeks before and claimed that Earl looked terrible. He had been sent to jail for some crime, and while he was there he had been raped and was now a "flaming queen." A few years after that, I was told Earl died of AIDS.

In order to survive the mental and physical damage I endured, I threw myself into a deeper level of emotional shutdown. From that point on, I cut my feelings off completely. Dorothy, as well as the entire community, seemed to be telling me that I had no value as a person. As I perceived it, my body didn't matter to anyone and my pain would last forever.

Within me, Miss Hyde determined that no one could touch "our" inner self again, no matter what they did to "us." Later I found out that many children who are victims of abuse and rape establish a dual personality to help them escape from all the devastation in their lives. In my case, I was aware that Miss Hyde had been with me since I was five years old. My heart had gradually become cold and hard toward men and any women like my mother, and for survival purposes my pain had to be hidden away. Eventually, everything in life filtered through my fantasy world and the cruel world dimmed.

The only consolation I had for the entire episode, as well as my four years of high school, was the fact that along with my graduation came freedom. I was convinced I would finally be in charge of my own destiny and I determined to find a better way to live. Little did I know that in my shutdown mode, living would never be what it was meant to be.

Chapter 12

Graduating to the Unknown

I was crippled in many ways during my 1962 graduation events at Peabody High School. Most notably, I still suffered from pain in my knee. Besides my physical and emotional handicaps, no family would allow their son to associate with the daughter of a "dyke," so I had no date for the prom or the graduation party. Of course, everyone knew I had been raped by an older guy, and the consensus around campus was that I encouraged it to happen.

Even though the graduation ceremony represented a major accomplishment because of all I had been through, it was also a very lonely time for me because I had no one with whom to share it.

True to form, Dorothy failed to show up at the ceremony, nor did she bother to congratulate me. It was clear Dorothy wanted nothing to do with me, but she did shock me by paying for my senior pictures. The force behind that decision came from the woman she was living with at the time. She insisted Dorothy should pay for them, and to make sure the task was done, the woman gave Dorothy half the money. My "Uncle" Bobby bought my dress and I think my Aunt Ruthie paid for my shoes. In comparison to my eighth-grade graduation, I didn't play a star role and I certainly wasn't anyone's princess!

I was hoping for a scholarship to go on to college, and had talked to the counselor about applying, but all of the applications required Dorothy's signature and financial statements. She refused to give out any of this information.

As I had done in the past, I could have forged her signature, but I had no way of obtaining her job history or the financial data they requested. As for myself, I had never been able to work while in high school because nobody would believe I was sixteen years old. They all asked for my birth certificate to verify my age, but Dorothy refused to tell me where it was. She wouldn't even consider making a copy of it for my use to get a work permit. Perhaps she didn't even know where it was because we had to leave the house on South Euclid.

The only other person I could consult was my grandmother. However, Grandmere, by this time, had lost most of her ability to hold on to reality for any length of time, and even with her best effort she couldn't remember where Dorothy may have placed my birth certificate. She had lost all her bearings as she went back and forth living at all her children's houses.

Finally I had another piece of paper which would work for me. With my diploma in hand, at last I could apply for work. Not long after graduation, I was able to find a job at a hospital working with the special dietary unit. I was thrilled to be making some money of my own for the first time in my life.

I also made a decision to do something I had wanted to do since I was five years old. After talking to my former foster parents, the Williams, they agreed to let me move back in with them with the understanding that I would pay something for my room and board. Mom Williams explained this was necessary to help me learn to be an adult, so we had a tearful reunion and they welcomed me with loving arms. My salary began rolling in and life was good for the first time since I had been forced to leave their home in 1950.

When I was a child, the Williams had taken me to Virginia each summer for a week's vacation. This time I was thrilled about joining them once again on their trip, and it was wonderful seeing my old friends who were now grown up like me. We all partied and had an exhilarating reunion.

After we returned home, I met a man named William Kemp who was ten years my senior. Immediately I dropped his first name and from then on referred to him as Kemp, but he wasn't exactly the man of my dreams as far as looks were concerned. Instead of being devastatingly handsome, as all my romance novels indicated was a prerequisite, he had a medium build with dark hair and brown eyes.

I was impressed, however, that Kemp was always a sharp dresser and was nice to me. It was a bonus that he was a fairly successful real estate salesman. When I really think about it, the most notable attribute Kemp possessed was the fact that he never mentioned Dorothy and didn't seem to be concerned with my background.

Kemp would often pick me up from work and take me out to dinner. We visited his friends, enjoyed bowling, and went to the drive-in on weekends. At the time, it didn't bother me in the least that he was separated from his wife and twin girls. I was totally cut off from my feelings and I was sure I wasn't worthy of spending time with a single man.

Even when Kemp began to make sexual advances after six months or so, in my mind he never really "touched" me. I was never excited about Kemp, and no matter what he said or did, I did not experience emotional intimacy. There was simply no fulfillment in making love with him, but then again, I never knew there was such a thing as pleasure in regards to sex.

As I got to know more about Kemp, I realized he was a mommy's boy and was spoiled to death. That reason alone was probably why his first marriage didn't last. He was separated from his wife after only ten days of marriage. Conveniently, his father was a policeman and always seemed to take care of "things" for the record so Kemp didn't have to support his wife who ended up delivering twins. Still, for the first time since Johnny had walked out of my life, someone wanted to be with me and I considered this to be quite an accomplishment.

When I started getting involved with Kemp, I made a daring decision. I had just turned eighteen and I made up my mind it was time to find a place of my own. Even though I loved the Williams dearly, many things had changed since I had been forced to leave their house in 1950. Instead of being a little girl needing guidance, now I was a young woman who had seen too much to be told what to do and how to do it.

For the first time in my life I was starting to save money, and I realized I was making enough from my job at the hospital to cover additional expenses. I found a room in a house in nearby Homestead, Pennsylvania, and the Williams were supportive of my next step toward adulthood. I felt like I was making great advances.

My neatly furnished room was very large and cheery and I shared a bathroom and the kitchen. It was perfect! I could even stop by to visit my foster parents and we got along even better than when I lived with them. Maybe this was because I felt better about myself, and we were able to discuss the painful years when I had yearned for Mom Williams to come to my rescue. She explained that she knew she couldn't interfere in my life, and she shared how she had suffered from my loss. It helped me find peace when I better understood what she had gone through.

One day, my brother Reggie telephoned me and told me he had not eaten all day. He was staying with Dorothy and her new girlfriend, and there was no food in the house. Reggie had been forbidden to see me or talk to me since Dorothy had dragged him away from Bert's house that cold October night two years ago. He was now ten years old. I told him to meet me at a certain restaurant and promised to treat him to a good meal.

While we ate, Reggie and I had much to catch up on. He told me about Dorothy's new friend named Jenny. She was white with blond hair and was very nice to my brother. We also talked about how he was getting along in school. I told him I would get paid the next day, so he was to come back again to meet me at the restaurant. I wanted to give him money to keep for himself so he could eat every day.

This was the first time he had the courage to seek me out for help, and I knew he was taking a big chance. Unfortunately, my worst fears came true. Somehow Dorothy found out that he had seen me, and she beat him so severely that Jenny became frightened. Jenny found my phone number and called to let me know what was happening to Reggie because she was concerned that Dorothy would really hurt him.

I can't remember how I got to the flat that night, but I know Dorothy was beating him when I arrived. As I reached the downstairs entry, I could hear his screams coming from the second floor. When Dorothy saw me bolt to the top of the stairs, she shouted profanities in my direction to intimidate me. In any confrontation, it was always her strategy to strike fear into my heart with words.

Dorothy spit out her words with venom. "What the heck are you doing here, witch? You want some of what I just gave your brother?"

With Miss Hyde's tenacity, I stepped up to her face. "Yes, if you think you're capable of dealing with a grown-up! Or maybe your specialty is beating defenseless children?"

She listened, although her stance was defiant.

I hesitated a moment to allow my question to sting, but I couldn't hold back for long. I stood tall to try to appear bigger than I was at ninety-eight pounds. "I'm not young anymore, and I'm just waiting for you to act like you want to beat me because tonight I promise I'll kill you!"

Dorothy backed up, dropped the belt, pivoted and stomped back into her living room in a rage. This time she took her anger out on Jenny. "Just what did you think you were doing when you phoned Jakii?" she lashed out. "I know you ratted, and it's none of your darn business!"

In order to protect Jenny, I quickly stepped in between them and continued my threat. "Remember, if you ever hit my brother again, I'll find you no matter where you are and I will personally kill you!" Miss Hyde's rage continued to give me strength. "You have no excuse to beat Reggie because he was hungry and came to me for help. And, in case you're thinking about punishing Jenny, you'd better think again because I'll call the police and report you for drug trafficking."

Dorothy's eyes widened.

"And I won't stop there," I brazenly continued. "I'll call your drug lord and tell him you're stealing from him."

Now I had Dorothy's attention. She knew I never made threats I did not keep! The truth was, no matter what I said to Dorothy, I would have gone out of my way to actually avoid fighting her because I had seen so much violence on 200 South

Euclid when I was growing up. My grandfather would argue with Grandmere and beat her up, and other renters in the house would beat their wives or girlfriends. Dorothy was always fighting with one of her lovers, and so I had come to hate violence and fighting on any level.

I didn't even like to argue because of the bad memories I carried from my past. One day during the six-day marriage between Dorothy and Cleophas, he and one of his friends were drinking at Grandmere's house while watching a fight on TV. When their dispute began, Cleophas sent me down the hall to get something. By the time I returned, they were throwing blows at each other. Cleophas punched his friend in the face just as I stepped back into the room, and the blood splattered all over my dress. I screamed and ran from the room. After that, I made it a point to avoid men who drank, and decided I would never fight unless I was forced into a situation.

In defense of Reggie, I was prepared to do some major damage to Dorothy, but she quickly backed away and locked herself in another room until after I left. Dorothy didn't say another word, and I ended my threat with a tone of finality. "Let me make it known that Reggie is free to call me whenever he wants, and especially when he's hungry!"

Many years later Reggie and I talked about the incident. He claimed Dorothy never touched him again, but she continued to do a lot of yelling and threatening. That was typical "Dorothy."

A month after the big confrontation, I received a visit from a local police officer. I was being summoned to the station in connection with the theft and sale of savings bonds. I phoned Kemp's father, the policeman, and he told me he would look into the problem. He also made it clear that I still needed to go with the officer.

Thankfully, the detective only questioned me and let me go. Eventually I found out Dorothy had filed charges against me for supposedly stealing her savings bonds and cashing them in. I never knew Dorothy even had bonds, and I had not lived with her for over two years. Just how was I supposed to know about and have access to them?

The investigation finally revealed the bonds had been cashed, but they had Dorothy's signature on them! The whole episode was an attempt by Dorothy to get even with me for threatening her about Reggie's safety and making her look bad in front of Jenny. Dorothy did have her ways! Even though I lived clear across town from her, I still wasn't far enough away from her anger.

Chapter 13

New Location / Old Baggage

Fairfax, a neighborhood in Los Angeles. . . 1963 - 1966

I can't say I was ever in love with William Kemp because I had no idea what real love was all about. I could never feel about him the same way I had felt about Johnny, but then again, at this point in my life I didn't "feel" much of anything. I was an expert at blocking out pain and focusing on survival. Kemp was simply someone who voluntarily chose to spend time with me.

I had barely moved into my new place when Kemp announced he was moving to California to start his own new life. Kemp confessed he had already made plans to move in with his brother and sister in Los Angeles, and he promised he would send for me if I wanted to join him. Now I had another major decision to make.

It didn't take long to make up my mind. *What do I have to lose?* I asked myself. *Nothing is holding me to Pittsburgh.*

Despite my long-winded threat to Dorothy concerning

Reggie, she truly had forbidden him to ever see me again or even speak my name in her presence. All my aunts and uncles had their own lives, and I was eager to take a brave step forward and walk away from the memories of my past. Somehow I believed as long as I was in charge of my own life, I would never let anyone hurt me the way my family and friends had done for so many years.

So in the summer of 1963, a year after I had graduated from Peabody High School, I boarded a bus to Los Angeles, California. For someone who had only traveled through a few states on the East Coast, I never dreamed the expanse of our country was so vast! Days went by as the bus wound through the Midwest and the western United States, but as far as my feelings were concerned, I remained numb.

Still, each day of driving assured at least a physical barrier between myself and my past. When I finally arrived in Los Angeles, Kemp met me at the bus station and took me to his little apartment. Early on, I found a job working as a live-in nanny in Westwood, and this was to be the beginning of a whole new life for me. I never mentioned my real family back in Pittsburgh to anyone. As far as I was concerned, I had a clean slate.

The first major obstacle presented itself when I missed my second menstrual period. Kemp and I were certainly not married, and he was none too happy to have another baby on the way. He had already deserted his wife and two daughters in Pittsburgh, and still refused to support them. I was always the one who sent money to Kemp's mother so she could buy things the twins needed. Now, with my own pregnancy, I should have known the predicament into which I had gotten myself. From the time Kemp found out about my condition, he went out of his way to make my life a living hell.

I truly did not get pregnant on purpose. All my life I had been taking care of one relative or another's children and I was glad to be free of that responsibility. So I was not too happy about it either in the beginning, but I learned to enjoy the prospect of having a baby. Kemp never did get excited about it.

I never expected Kemp to marry me, but as a stranger in a new environment, I felt I had to make our relationship work. In order to make more money, I resigned my position as a nanny and temporarily moved in with Kemp's sister. Soon I found a job working for the telephone company and a few months later, Kemp and I were able to move into a small, one-bedroom apartment over a garage in the Fairfax area of Los Angeles.

Unfortunately, my money-making idea went up in smoke when all the pregnant women at the telephone company were ordered to leave because someone there had reported an outbreak of the German measles. In order to keep paying the rent, we still needed to make extra money, so Kemp's sister came to the rescue. She made an arrangement to place a bookie for a horse-racing operation in our tiny dining room, and our cut of the money paid for our rent.

Kemp was now selling insurance. He would leave home by seven-thirty in the morning and didn't return until about one or two the next morning. I never knew what mood he would be in when he came home, but I always braced myself. Sometimes he would try to wake me and say, "Get up! I'm going to punch that darn baby out of you!" He was such a sweetheart!

One morning as Kemp left for work, I made a request. "Could you please come home at lunchtime and bring me a sandwich or some money so I can eat?" He knew that we had very little food in the pantry and it was his payday.

"I'll think about it!" was his curt reply as he rushed out the door. Kemp telephoned me later that afternoon and said that

. he and some people from work were going out for drinks.

"I really don't care," I said in a matter-of-fact way. "But before you go, could you please bring me something to eat? You know I haven't eaten all day!"

He told me what I could kiss and hung up the phone. Now I was really angry! Here I was, six months pregnant with his child, and no family of my own to turn to. I was in a new city and state with no car or money. I felt helpless—I was despondent! I already knew his brother didn't care about me because he and Kemp had long ago discussed how and why I should sign myself into a shelter for unwed mothers and give up the child for adoption.

Sometimes his brother would call the apartment and invite Kemp to a party without any mention of including me. Naturally, I was hurt, and when I asked Kemp about it, he would tell me it was not his place to invite me if his brother didn't want me there. "After all," Kemp flippantly explained, "it's not my party, so what can I do?" The end result was that most of the time I was alone because, during the time we could have been together, Kemp would usually go to events or parties without me.

With this in mind, I made a clear-cut decision that day he stranded me at home; I simply was not going to take that treatment from him! With all the fervor of a mad woman, I went down to the garage, brought up a can of gasoline, grabbed a book of matches and sat at the front door to wait for Kemp to arrive home. I was single minded! During the hours I waited intently with the lights out and no music, I didn't move from my spot of attack except to go to the bathroom.

All the while I seethed inside because I knew Kemp very well. He never drank, smoked, played cards, gambled, or hung out with the guys. He only had one vice: if he was out, he was certainly with one or more females. In fact, I already knew he was sleeping with a woman from the front apartment building of our complex.

Late that night, Kemp walked up the stairs to our front door, slid his key into the lock, and opened the door. I sprang into action and dowsed him thoroughly with gasoline. By the time I reached for the matches, he had already jumped over the porch railing and was racing through the parking lot. Of course, I laughed until my sides hurt! When Kemp finally did weasel back home early the next morning, he came with an offering of food. I found it interesting how he never again left me without groceries or money as long as we were together.

When I went into labor with my first child on the morning of August 10, 1964, I was twenty years old. Kemp was now working for a bus company and I awakened him at five in the morning to let him know the time had come. When he phoned my doctor's office, they told him to time my pains and call back. My contractions were between fifteen and twenty minutes apart, so the doctor said it was time to bring me into the hospital. Void of any enthusiasm, Kemp went into the bathroom, took a shower, shaved, washed his hair and went through all of his usual morning routine as if nothing was happening.

While he was prepping, I reminded him to make sure and bring the money we had set aside to pay for my hospital stay. His flat reply almost made me deliver the baby on the spot. "There's no money. I spent it all."

There I was sitting on the bed in labor, realizing this man was basically telling me that I would have to go to a county hospital because we had no money! I tried to stay calm and telephoned my doctor again to explain what Kemp had just told me. I asked the doctor if he could go to the county hospital to deliver my child, but his answer was, "No." At least he did tell me to follow up with him after the delivery, and he would call ahead to the county hospital to talk to the appropriate doctor on duty and fill him in on my case.

By the time we arrived, my labor pains were ten to twelve minutes apart. They had just enough time to load me on a table for a quick exam, then whisk me through the x-ray machines and into the labor room. The doctor came in, introduced himself, and in the same breath yelled for a nurse to get me into delivery. The doctor distinctively said, "Don't push!" However, my son Durksen had other ideas and came out running.

At that glorious moment, Kemp was nowhere to be found. He had dropped me off at the emergency room that Monday morning and then immediately left the hospital. I didn't see him again until he checked with me on Tuesday afternoon, and then again he showed up late on Wednesday to take us home. When we arrived at the apartment, he put up the crib, laid down on the sofa and finally had something to say. "What's for dinner?"

The whole situation reminded me of something Dorothy had said to me when I was young. "You're worthless, and you'll never amount to anything." At that moment, I truly felt like a pathetic non-entity whom no one wanted. I also had an unwanted baby that only I cared about. I knew that I loved my son and somehow I knew he was safe to love. At one time I had thought Kemp was a safe person to care about and that he cared about me, but now I realized that I had left Pittsburgh only to fall back into the same familiar pit of feeling unwanted and unprotected.

A few months later Kemp moved us into a larger apartment. We still had only one bedroom, but at least there was more square footage. Kemp enjoyed telling me how ugly I was and reminded me how grateful I should be that he decided to stick it out with me. Certainly no other man would want a woman with a child, he informed me. Of course, I believed him.

I felt certain that I was financially unable to make it on my own, so our life continued to be a tug of war. Kemp was never without a female or two during this time of our living together, and he would even come home from the market with telephone numbers written on the grocery bag. His explanation was that the numbers were totals of what he had purchased. Excuse me! With only two or three items in the bag, there was no way the price would add up to all of those numbers. He obviously didn't care enough about me to make the effort to hide his lies.

Kemp's next decision was to put me on a food budget of two dollars a day. This huge sum was to pay for his breakfast, lunch and dinner. Even in the mid-1960s, not a lot could be done with two dollars. I already had experience with this type of problem with Dorothy, so I worked it all out for him—oh yes, you can believe I did!

For breakfast I bought him corn flakes and milk, but there was no sugar. For lunch he had a dry bologna and bread without any mustard, mayonnaise or cheese. His dinner consisted of beans and Kool Aid, minus the sugar. The poor man complained that he required sugar on his cereal, and wondered if I would be a decent shopper and buy him a few hot dogs for his dinner. He insisted on having at least some sort of meat.

"No problem," I sweetly retorted while maintaining a straight face. Later that evening I went to the store and purchased sugar for his cereal and hotdogs for his dinner. However, now he was missing milk for his cereal and there was no bologna to top his bread and mustard for lunch. For dinner he lacked beans to go with his hotdog wrapped in one slice of bread, but his Kool-Aid did contain sugar!

He was furious. His look of disgust registered off the scale as he stood looking at his scrumptious dinner. Of course, the baby and I had already eaten, and we certainly didn't eat beans. If he really wanted to spend two dollars a day for food, I was certainly willing to accommodate him! Now he declared he wanted to see milk and sugar on the table for his breakfast and meat in his lunch.

Promptly the next morning I poured milk in his cereal bowl and added the sugar, but left out the corn flakes just as he had requested. For lunch I squirted mustard on top of his bologna and wrapped it in foil instead of bread. I still laugh today when I remember some of the looks on his face during that week. They were priceless!

After this experience with my gourmet cooking on only two dollars a day, he quickly changed his tune. However, I also saw clearly that in order for the baby and me to survive, I had to secure a job and buy a car. I would probably have to pay for child care myself. Once I found a job again, Kemp came up with a unique idea on how to punish me for working overtime. He locked me out of the apartment! His idea was, if he wanted me there, I was supposed to be there.

It didn't take much time to realize that my life with Kemp strangely paralleled my life with Dorothy. The only time I had fun was when I wasn't with him. He seemed to enjoy making me suffer by putting me down, calling me names, and finding reasons to criticize and sabotage me no matter what I did. For the longest time I had no clue how to get beyond him in my life.

One day a neighbor named Cynthia asked if I would model for her. She was a student at a beauty college in Los Angeles and was looking for a subject to practice on to prepare for her boards. I discussed it with Kemp, and he responded with an emphatic, "No!" Of course, immediately I agreed to do it!

Cynthia's husband was a milkman, and Kemp always tried to

make me believe that it was her husband who was really interested in me. Even though Kemp had never met my mother, he tried hard to make me believe that I was a slut and would accuse my mother of also being one. This cut into my pain like a knife, and it also annoyed me. He never cared to find out much about Dorothy when we first started going out in Pittsburgh, and now he wanted to slice up her reputation. Who did he think he was? Still, I knew not to believe Kemp's crazy ideas about Cynthia's husband, and besides, she was absolutely beautiful.

Kemp would always insist that I was making eyes at some man. To avoid stirring up trouble with him, even if we were attending a party together, I would scout around for an isolated spot, get a soft drink to sip and sit there all night in silence. On the other hand, Kemp was a social butterfly. He danced and talked with every woman in the place except me.

Inevitably, some man would always find his way over to me and ask me to dance. I'd refuse, but if he stayed around to talk with me, Kemp assumed I had encouraged him. I was always the one at fault. Strangely enough, when I had lived with Dorothy, I was always the one at fault as well. According to her, I should have been able to stop what was happening, made something different happen, or I should have somehow handled the situation differently. Again, here I was with Kemp who treated me the same way.

My whole approach to Kemp, and the negative influence he had on my life, changed one night when I was talking to Cynthia. The conversation began while she was shampooing my hair. "Why don't I ever see you smile, Jakii?"

I was too stunned by her question to reply.

"You're young, pretty, and you seem to be very smart. So why are you always sad?" she went on.

"I'm not sad," I meekly replied.

"Girl, that long face you're wearing every time you walk in here certainly doesn't look like a smile to me!" she teased.

I stared at her for a second because no one had ever told me I looked sad. "I bet your old man tells you you're fat and ugly, and no other man would want you since you've had your little boy."

She had my attention now!

"Trust me, he just wants you to feel insecure and afraid to go anywhere. I bet when you go out, he makes you sit in a corner and won't allow you to talk to anyone! Am I right?" she insisted on knowing.

It was as if Cynthia had been in our apartment or riding in the car when Kemp had said and done all of those things to me. "How did you know?" I muttered in amazement.

"Oh, girl, that was an easy one! It's because of how I met your husband."

"You've met Kemp?" I gasped.

"I was out shopping and he tried to flirt with me!" she quipped. "All I had to do was tell him that my husband was a very big man and that he was just one aisle over in the store. Your old man took off, but when we were leaving the market, I saw him get into his car."

Could this have really been Kemp? I wondered.

"As my husband and I pulled into our complex, we saw him pull up across the street," Cynthia elaborated. "At first I thought he was bold enough to follow us, but after I saw him park and walk up the steps, I knew he must be a neighbor."

She kept talking and I didn't want to miss a word.

"Then one day I saw the two of you leaving the house carrying a baby, and I guessed the rest. Remember the day it was raining and your car broke down? My husband saw you and the baby and gave you a lift home." I nodded as I did remember the occasion.

"Well, my husband told me how nice you were and wondered why you were so sad," she concluded.

Does everybody see me as a depressed, washed-out woman? I wondered. The question was actually a weighty revelation. My mouth fell wide open.

While she set my hair, Cynthia reaffirmed that I didn't have to stay with someone like Kemp. "Your old man is such a piece of crap, girl! I'm going to give you some advice. If you ever decide to leave him and don't have a place to go, you and your baby are always welcome in our house until you find a place of your own."

"How do you know all of this will work?"

She barely took a breath. "My husband tried to put some of that stuff on me once, and I just got up and left him! When he found me, he begged me to come back. We had a long talk and laid down some rules. One of them was that if he ever thought he had to put me down again, then I was out of his life forever." She stood up and looked me in the eye. "I told him I really loved him, but I wasn't going to let any man make me feel I was dirt for him to walk on! Honey, he's been straight ever since then and we really have a good marriage now."

I considered her well-timed message, but I also had a burning question. "Do you think I can really make it on my own with a baby to support?" I quizzed her.

"Heck, of course you can!" was her confident comeback.

Once I was under the hair dryer, I had time to think. Her advice replayed over and over in my head. Cynthia was the first person in a long time who had words of encouragement for me. The fact that she knew what I was going through was a revelation in itself.

Previously, when I had voiced doubts about Kemp to one of his family members about the way he treated me, I was always told the problem was "in my mind." They reminded me I should be grateful that Kemp was willing to take care of me and my baby. The words, "My baby. . .my baby!" ripped through me like a dagger. What about the fact that Kemp was the father of "my baby"?

I also thought of his family's other catch phrase: "You should be glad he's providing you a place to live!" That wasn't true, either. I was working hard and contributing more than half of everything. On top of that, he refused to pay for the babysitter.

An idea began forming in my mind. *Maybe I can leave him. If I can work and pay half the bills and all my own necessities, then I should be able to pay my own expenses somewhere else.* After all, I took care of my brother Reggie and myself when I was only twelve years old, so what would be the difference now? By the time my hair was finished, I knew I was going to leave Kemp.

When I arrived home, I was one joyful woman. As I put the baby to bed, I remembered a promise that I had made to myself when I was under Dorothy's oppression. Just as I vowed to survive and escape from Dorothy, I knew that I would soon be free of Kemp. I would make it without him. I also knew it would take some planning, financially and logistically, but it would just be a matter of a few months.

When Kemp came home that night, immediately he noticed my change of disposition. "Just where have you been and what have you been doing?" he demanded.

"You know I was at the beauty school," I replied with a defiant grin.

"Then what are you smiling about?" He just couldn't give it up. "You don't look that great to be smiling about your hair! In fact, I'm not going to let you go back there again!"

I laughed and paraded into the bathroom to get ready for bed. I knew I would have some rough spots ahead, but I would wait until the perfect timing and make my break. *Baby, I'm out of here!* played over and over in my head.

One day after work, one of my co-workers told me about a wonderful store with great prices on infant clothing. She, too, had a young baby and knew where to find the bargains. Kemp and I were going to attend a company picnic that weekend, and I had just been paid. So, I thought I'd take some time after work to buy my son a few outfits. I took the bus home that evening, and when I walked through our door I discovered Kemp had taken all of my clothes out of the closets and had thrown them on the bed and floor.

In stunned disbelief, I blurted out, "Just what's going on here?"

"You and your baby, get the heck out of my house!" he spit out. "You can go back to your 'dyke' mother and the street where you belong, for all I care!"

In a split second my whole life flashed before me. I remembered all the years of being called names and being told I was not wanted. I remembered sleeping from sofa to floor in other people's homes, days of being hungry and cold and always having to take care of someone else's children. All of these things flashed before my eyes, and I lost control.

Even though I knew I wanted to leave Kemp, we ended up having a huge fight that night. At that time I weighed only ninety-two pounds and was no match for him. I ended up physically abused, but in the end I didn't care. I was furious because no one was going to force me to leave a place when I was helping to make the payments for it.

After the fight, I went into the bathroom, washed the blood off my face, changed my clothes and calmly asked Kemp what he wanted for dinner. He was beaming with the look of power and his chest was puffed with pride. As he strutted around the apartment, he was spouting off what he expected from me from that day on. But I wasn't even listening!

Later that night, after he fell asleep, I abruptly woke him up. I was sitting on his chest, my knees were up near his neck and I had a large knife pressed against his throat. Now I had his attention. "If you ever hit me again, I'll cut you up in small pieces and send you home to your mother!" Miss Hyde had spoken again.

To make an even deeper impression, I cut his neck just enough to let him know I meant business. He jumped out of bed and never came back in the bedroom to join me. The same held true for other nights when he knew he had treated me badly. He would either sit up wide awake in a living room chair or stay out all night.

I was forced to seriously contemplate my situation. All my life, the people who were supposed to love me had treated me like a rag to be used at their will and finally to be thrown away. "Well, no more!" I decided. I had reached my limit, and this time I was ready for a real change.

Chapter 14

On My Own At Last

Finally, my big day arrived. As usual, I woke up before Kemp and took the baby to the sitter's house. Kemp went to work, and then I drove back home. I had scheduled a moving van and paid for a new apartment. By five o'clock that evening when Kemp was due to come home, I had moved into my own place. I had everything set up, including my bed and the baby's crib, the boxes were unpacked and I had shopped for a few groceries.

When Kemp discovered I was gone, he ran straight to Cynthia's house to find out what I had done. According to Cynthia's report, Kemp tried to accuse her of moving me out, but her husband showed up and ran him off like a scared puppy. It actually took Kemp a day or two to muster up the nerve to call me at work and ask where I was staying with "his" baby.

"Your baby?" I retaliated. "Of all the nerve!" All of Kemp's family members, who never cared to help me, were now calling and telling me how wrong I was for taking my baby away from his father.

"What chance is there to think you can make it out there on

your own with some other man's child? After all," they surmised, "no other man would want you!" All of this sounded very familiar.

Thankfully, I proved them all wrong because my son and I did make it. However, for the most part, life in my twenties continued in the same pattern. I would enter relationships, be the loving, giving person they expected for a while, and then one day they would do something to hurt me. Suddenly they would find themselves face-to-face with a fire-breathing dragon who had no fear of death. I thought I had to remain tough in order to survive, but there was also a softer side of me that I was afraid to show to anyone other than my son Durksen.

No matter what my circumstances were, for two or three years after arriving in California, I always sent money to my brother Reggie so he would have lunch money or something to eat despite his situation with Dorothy. On his birthdays I sent cards with money enclosed. It was never much, and varied from five to twenty dollars, but I always added a note asking him to write me to let me know how he was doing. However, I never heard a word back from him.

In late May 1968, five years after I had moved to Los Angeles, I was shocked to receive a letter from Reggie. Actually, it was an invitation to attend his high school graduation. He also enclosed a note informing me that since he had not heard from me since my departure from Pittsburgh, he really didn't care if I came or not.

What a little brat! I thought.

He explained that he had several other people to invite if I didn't want to attend. *He hasn't contacted me for all these years and yet somehow has the nerve to address me this way?* I was hurt and dumbfounded. I telephoned him and asked why he decided to send me such a nasty note. His answer made sense after it sunk in. It became quite obvious that Dorothy had never bothered to give him my cards or letters because they all mentioned I had enclosed some money for him. He had never received any of the money I had sent to him. Dorothy even told him that I had to leave town because I was going to be arrested for stealing her bonds, and for prostitution, as well.

I went into shock as he explained his side of the story, but after considering the source, I knew Reggie was telling me what he thought was the truth. Good old Dorothy had struck again. She had even resorted to lying to her own son in order to downgrade me in his eyes. Reggie didn't know the charges against me concerning the bond had been dismissed immediately when Jenny told the truth to the police. Also, it was painful to have my brother think of me as a prostitute and I knew I had to go home to straighten things out in person.

I found a good friend to care for my son while I was gone, and when I arrived in Pittsburgh, I freshened up and immediately took a cab to Dorothy's apartment. My plan was to confront her and tell her what I thought of her tactics. But I wasn't prepared in the slightest for her response. I determined to come across as an adult and an equal, and as I knocked on her door, I confidently gave my name when she inquired who was there.

"Jakii Edwards," I answered back.

"Well, who is Jakii Edwards?" she countered.

"Your daughter, Jakii." I knew her lack of acknowledgment was really weird and I couldn't wait to report back to my therapist.

Finally, Dorothy opened the door just a crack to see who I was. She peeped around the door and asked again, "Who are you?"

"My name is Jakii, and I'm R.G.'s and Alma's granddaughter and Reggie's sister," I elaborated.

Dorothy just stood and looked me up and down for a while.

She never really opened the door for me.

"Is Reggie here?" I calmly asked.

"No, he went to the rehearsal for his graduation."

"Well, may I come in and wait for him?" I moved closer to the crack in the door.

"I guess so," was her bland reply. She opened the door, turned and walked back into the living room. Without looking at me she sat down in a chair to light her joint. I came in and waited by the door. She didn't offer me a seat, so I stood until she acknowledged my presence and finally offered me a chair. "So you're Reggie's sister?" she repeated as though it still was not sinking in. I thought her response was a crazy one to make to her own child, but I counseled myself by remembering that this was Dorothy and why should I expect more?

The entire time I was in Dorothy's house that day, she never truly professed to know me. Later Reggie told me she announced to him that his sister had come by to see him, but to my face she refused to recognize me as her daughter. We made some polite conversation about Reggie's commencement exercises and the time they were scheduled to begin. I asked her about her health, and she said a few things, but finally I couldn't hold back my anger any longer.

This was the opportunity Miss Hyde and I had been waiting for. It was easy to blast Dorothy about how I had felt during all the years she had abandoned Reggie and me. I demanded to know why she chose to leave me alone with a young child to raise while she partied with her friends and lovers. Also, I insisted on knowing if she ever loved us and why she had always put her lovers and their families before her own children. She delivered no answers.

Still, I wasn't finished with Dorothy. I told her I was doing just fine considering the fact that I was a mental wreck now, thanks to all the years of abuse I had suffered while living with her. Truthfully, I had been wrapped up in so much rage from my upbringing, I had suffered a breakdown and was currently under the treatment of a psychologist.

I yearned for Dorothy to understand that I wanted to love her like normal children love their parents, but because she had treated me so cruelly, it was still impossible for me to ever forgive her. Still, those poignant points were not enough to unload on Dorothy. "My main problem, thanks to you, is I don't know how to love anyone at all!"

It was like talking to a wall. I left her house that day without any additional insight, but I felt about two thousand pounds lighter. When I returned to my counseling sessions, the first thing my therapist asked was, "What happened to you? You look fantastic!"

I did get to spend time with my brother before leaving town, and we had a good talk about all the things I had and had not done when I was caring for him. It was good to straighten things out, but it took quite a while. He was angry because he felt I should have written him, and he even wanted to know why I hadn't sent for him.

In calm and loving tones, I told him about all the cards and letters, and the money I had sent him from each of my paychecks. I explained how I had instructed my employers to set aside a certain amount each payday which would not go into my check. Sometimes I earned extra money babysitting so I would have a little more to send him. Poor Reggie was in shock when he realized why he had never received a dime. He needed to know I had also been hurt when he failed to call or send me a thank-you note.

Once the air was cleared, our bond was stronger than ever. When we told Aunt Bar about the things Dorothy had accused me of, she laughed and told Reggie what I was really like. I had always told her everything. As far as the prostitution charge, I explained to him that I only had one boyfriend named Charlie before I left with Kemp, and we were never intimate.

Sadly enough, my family never told the truth about anything unless they were forced to the point. Many of them knew who Reggie's dad was, but they kept quiet when Dorothy lied to Reggie about his identity. They never confronted Dorothy or made her accountable for her actions regarding us.

My aunts and uncles also knew that we were left alone in an apartment for nine to ten months out of the year, yet no one said a word to Dorothy about her neglect except for Bert. Dorothy's lovers knew the truth, too, but most of them treated us as if we were servants or orphans.

After our talk, Reggie confronted Dorothy about his father again, and she lied to him one more time. Finally, I encouraged him to seek out our uncles and question each one individually. Uncle Charles covered for Dorothy as usual, but finally Uncle Ray broke down and told my brother the truth about his dad. He even told Reggie where he might find him.

Uncle Ray was a bus driver and drove the bus Reggie's father took to work every week. He would ask Ray about Reggie, but Uncle Ray would never tell Reggie anything about him. Now the truth was finally out. Reggie located his father and they became close and were able to spend time together. This helped make up for a lot of hurt in Reggie's life.

Reggie also had quite a few things to tell me about the life he had to live without me. He revealed that he, too, had been awakened by strange noises when we were in bed with Dorothy and her "friends" when we were young. He confessed that he had been frightened and didn't want me to know what was going on, so he pretended to sleep and could do nothing but endure it.

Grandmere's condition had grown worse by the day, and when it was Dorothy's turn to care for her, she made Reggie stay home and tend to her. There were many hardships he had to bear alone, trying to take care of his grandmother when he was only 11 and 12 years of age. Having to watch out for an Alzheimer's patient is hard enough for a trained adult, much less for a young boy. Often there was no food, and when there was money for a McDonalds hamburger or two, he had to feed his grandmother first before he could eat.

Thankfully, he had found his father and I think that relationship did a lot toward building my brother as a man, even though they only had each other for a few years before his father died. Now, as an adult, Reggie had already turned into a wonderful young man and we became very close.

Several years ago, I realized that having to care for Reggie as a child gave me a purpose to stay alive and kept me from doing many silly things.

After that amazing week in Pittsburgh, I returned home to my son. For the next three years I continued to work and care for him as best as I could, and I also maintained relationships with married men. I honestly didn't believe anyone would ever love me for who I really was, so I settled for the unattainable. When it was time to end one of these relationships, I would not be surprised or hurt because the man had not been mine to begin with. I delivered another son named Scott in 1971, and shortly after his birth I had to have a hysterectomy.

I had been seeing a psychiatrist for years before Scott was born, but it was no big deal because everyone I knew in California had a "shrink." As I continued my therapy, pent-up anger inside of me kept surfacing. For some unknown reason, I could control parts of my body through the same "shut down" techniques I had been using in my mind to blot out painful memories for years. My doctors had already diagnosed me as suffering from a nervous breakdown, but now they suggested heavier therapy. I welcomed it, but I knew I was missing something very important in my life: I did not love myself!

For the most part, my heart had been hardened toward God because of my past, but in this deep desperation I knew that somehow I had to connect with the one true God. No one else was left to whom I could turn. Thus began my quest of searching through many religions. I had started out as a Catholic in Pittsburgh, but I was finished with priests. In California I explored the Jehovah's Witnesses, Judaism, Buddhism, and Agnosticism. This was no small task, and I spent many hours and even years studying their concepts and attending various congregations. But none of the groups met my needs or took hold of my soul.

By 1973 I was at the end of my rope in almost every way. The therapy sessions with my psychiatrists had ended, and although I was a little better, they didn't set me free from the pain in my heart and soul. My life seemed to be going nowhere. Even though I had found some good jobs, that overwhelming sense of worthlessness I had carried over from my childhood had never left me. Finally, I found myself seriously considering suicide.

Chapter 15

Do or Die

Culver City, California. . . 1973

There was one constant in my life besides my sons. About a year after I left Kemp and relocated, I made enough money to hire a gem of a housekeeper named Jewel. She showed up once a week for her regular duties, but her constant message was that I could have a new life with someone named Jesus Christ.

I knew who Jesus was, but I really didn't know what she was getting at. I wish I could say that I responded to her good news, but I only found it baffling. Over the years she watched as I explored many religions, but Jewel patiently kept telling me about a personal relationship I could have with Jesus.

My comeback to her had always been, "Okay, when I get too old to do anything but die, then I might think about it." In the meantime I thought, *If I don't bother God, maybe He won't mess with me!* Boy, was I wrong! I needed Him much sooner than I expected.

On the evening of September 13, 1973, I was alone in my

bedroom. It was around ten o'clock and was by far the darkest night of my life. No one could have guessed by looking at me, but I wanted to check out of the heartache known as life, and I was getting ready to make my big exit. Here I was, twenty-nine years old, with two beautiful sons and a good job. I was still thin and attractive. To my advantage, I had made it standard practice to only date wealthy men who were generous. Serious drugs or alcohol had never touched my lips, and I didn't gamble or stay out all week partying. Whenever I had to go out of town, I left my children with someone very reliable such as Jewel or one of my friends who had children. I took classes to better my education, and as far as the world was concerned, I was a successful woman.

I had just moved into a beautiful, newly built apartment in a then small town known as Culver City, California. But despite my outward credentials, I hated myself. My fantasy world could no longer cover up the real world I faced, which was filled with pain and inner conflict, and I couldn't fight the war within myself anymore.

This particular night I didn't waste any time in my usual pity-party mode because I knew exactly what I was going to do. In one hand I had four or five potent pills, which I had borrowed from a friend because I never had anything stronger than aspirin in my own home. In my other hand I had a to-do list of errands I had to run before taking my life that night. I sat on the side of my bed to verify that I had covered all the details. On the back side was another list containing last-minute possibilities for the direction of my life.

As far as I was concerned, I only had four options from which to choose: 1) commit suicide, 2) get married, 3) do drugs, and 4) try God. The pills were awaiting my choice of option number one. As far as option two, I couldn't think of anyone to marry.

Silly me, I realized, *they're already married!*

Option number three wasn't very satisfying, either. I already knew what drugs could do to people's lives. My stomach churned when I thought of the number of cars, houses, and bags of jewelry the drug dealers profited when they took advantage of other people's weaknesses. I enjoyed an occasional joint on my birthday or New Year's Eve, but all drug dealers would have been out of business if their fortunes had depended on me buying from them.

Because I quickly ruled out options two and three, the only options I had left were to commit suicide or try Jesus as Jewel had suggested. This was the designated night, so the pressure was on! In my frenzy of desperation, I finally decided I would first give this Jesus Christ a try. After all, if God wasn't all that He was cracked up to be, then I would still have the pills to implement option number one.

I set the pills aside on the night stand and threw my body across my bed to decide how I was going to go about this. I didn't have a clue about what to read in the Bible, so I just started talking to God. "If you're really out there, I ask you to hear my prayer!" There was silence, but I continued. "You know that Jewel told me about you. She said that Jesus could wipe my slate clean. According to her, I can start a new life with you."

As I spoke the words, I started to cry from the depths of my soul. I never would allow myself to cry, so this was radical for me. The thought that I was standing before God without any of my usual facades to protect me was more than I could take. If He was really out there, He was seeing me for who I really was, and that was both frightening and humbling at the same time! I could hardly go on, but somehow I pulled myself back together enough to continue.

"Oh, God, I'm so ugly and miserable! I don't even know who

you are, but Jewel said you would forgive me for my past sins. Believe me, I have millions of them!"

I was overwhelmed when I tried to recount some of the horrible things I had done and said to other people because of my own pain. As a child, I had been confused about sin. Talking back to my elders was a sin, telling the priest about my mother was a sin. As I saw it, almost everything I wanted to do when I attended the Catholic Church ended up being a sin. Now that I was an adult, the term took on all the darker sides of human nature. I sobbed with the heavy burden of my own sin weighing down upon me.

"God, Jewel told me you allowed your son, Jesus, to die on a cross long before I was born because you knew one day I would need a way out of the sin and pain I've been living with."

As I poured out my heart, I didn't expect any word from above. I just knew that I had to say everything Jewel had instructed. "God, I ask you into my life and heart tonight. I accept the price Jesus paid with His body on that cross as a payment for the life I've lived."

The next thing I knew, it was morning and the sun was shining through my bedroom window! I wasn't sure what had happened, but I had slept better than I had for more months than I could remember. The pills were still on my night stand, and the more I thought about it, nothing had actually happened.

Neither God nor Jesus had shown up to do any of the things Jewel said they would accomplish, and my life certainly didn't seem transformed. I wasn't sure what I really expected, but I suppose I was looking for some outward physical change. At least, that's the way I thought Jewel had told me it would be.

After the good rest, it wasn't hard to get ready for work that day. As usual, I parked in my designated spot in front of the home office of a large consumer finance company. My job description was administrative assistant to the head of personnel, and our department was in charge of hiring, firing, and employee reviews for the entire company. Everything had to filter across my desk before I presented it to my boss, and that morning I wasted no time jumping into the complexity of my day.

Everything was normal until I ran into some trouble with the main frame computer. I uttered some words in response to my frustration, and for the first time in my life I actually heard myself swear. That was interesting! I had never given any thought to the words coming out of my mouth before, but these words sounded simply horrible! *Wow, I wonder how often I do that?* I wondered. It really caught my attention, but I had no time to waste dwelling on this mystery.

The following week I was back at my desk working on a document when something happened to the tape that fed into the computer. It was maddening because I always had to stop to fix it, and sometimes I actually had to retype whatever I was working on because of the loss of data. This time I was frustrated, as usual.

"I can't believe this is happening to me again!" I fussed out loud. When I looked up, I saw several people standing around my desk staring at me. I couldn't help but ask, "What in the world is wrong with all of you?" I was still trying to straighten out the tape.

"You didn't swear!" one of the ladies exclaimed.

"So what? What's so strange about that?" I needed to know.

My boss was in the group and answered me. "Jakii, you always curse up a storm when something upsets you."

"And you've never been shy about it, either!" the accounting manager added.

I sat there stunned as they all walked away shaking their heads. Now I had the answer to the question I had asked myself that past week. I cursed all the time! Now I was really bothered. *How could I curse all the time without being aware of it? And, if I was notorious for my language, why did I stop now?* As I thought deeply about the whole situation, finally it dawned on me that something must have really happened inside of me that night when I asked Jesus to come into my heart!

At the close of the second week of my new life, one of the ladies who worked in payroll cornered me and began complaining about a certain employee. Sally was a bitter lady who constantly criticized everything and everyone, and she thought I should do something about this person in particular.

As I analyzed the situation with my new insight, I realized that normally my response would have been to curse her out and walk away. This time I listened to what she was saying without interrupting, and when she was finished, I told her that I would look into the matter. I ended the conversation by thanking her.

As I turned to walk away, I caught the look of astonishment on her face. I overheard her say to herself, "Well, I guess what they're saying about her is true. That Jesus stuff must really work!" After that she always stared at me, but never talked to me about a problem again. From that point on, I tried to give her a cheery greeting when we ran into each other in the halls. I discovered that I really wanted to change!

My boss was the first person to invite me to church. He and his wife attended Grace Church in Van Nuys, California, and the only thing I remember about the first service was the large wooden cross they had on the wall behind the altar. There must have been a light behind it because it gave off a very soft glow. It made the cross seem like a pillow where I could lay down and go to sleep. From the time I sat down in that church until we left, I could do nothing but cry.

Jewel, my housekeeper, also invited me to her church after I shared my experience with her. She was elated! I found her church service to be quite different. We arrived at ten in the morning and at one in the afternoon the pastor still didn't look like he was ready to get up to preach. They sang the same song over and over for about thirty minutes and people jumped and danced. For a new believer, that was too much and I decided their service was way too long. I never went back, but Jewel was so happy about my salvation that she honestly didn't mind if I chose another church to attend.

By the end of October 1973, I was attending a Bible study one night a week at my boss's home in Pacific Palisades. The following January, Pastor John MacArthur baptized me at Grace Church. I was overwhelmed with the significance of being cleansed of my sins and identifying with Christ, but some old hang-ups from my past caused me some concern.

I was afraid to go into the water because when I was young, Bert and Uncle Ray used to tell me stories about what happened when they baptized people. They said they would hold them under the water as long as it took to be sure all their sins were washed away. My sins were great, so I was afraid I might not ever make it out of the water!

There were lots of people being baptized along with me that day, and because my last name began with an "E," I was in the first group. I kept telling people they could go before me, and soon I found myself near the end of the line with my new friend Mary and her son whose last name began with a "S." Finally I went in and discovered it wasn't true about having to stay under water for such a long time. What a relief! I had a good laugh at myself that night after I got home.

As a new Christian, gradually I came face-to-face with many issues in my life which God wanted me to deal with. Only a few weeks after I had been saved, I met a man I called Mac and wondered if he was someone with whom I could have a relationship. I thought I was falling in love with Mac and he was constantly on my mind.

When I was studying the Bible one night, one word came strongly into my mind: "celibacy." I looked up the meaning and found it meant abstaining from sex. Someone in my Bible study group had mentioned that I should abstain from all sexual activity until I was married. I'd never heard anything like that before. They explained that sex outside of marriage was a sin. My first reaction had been, "Who cares?" However, during my Bible reading I ran across a verse that cleared my attitude up very quickly. Romans 6:23 said the wages of sin was death!

Since this was something I didn't want to hear, it made me ponder the authenticity of the Word of God. It took about two weeks of study and asking lots of questions to come to grips with the fact that the Bible was written by God through the inspiration of the Holy Spirit. If I believed God could forgive all my sins, then I had to believe all of what the Bible said. Either it was all true or all wrong. Once I was convinced beyond a doubt that it was all true, my next plan was to try to bargain with God.

I began talking to God as I walked all around my apartment. I assured Him I did believe in Him, but I reasoned that when His servants wrote the Bible, I was not yet born and He didn't know me yet. "God, I didn't get saved before I began having sex," I explained. "I already have two children and I'm just not used to being without a man. Can you just rethink this issue in regards to me?"

There was nothing but silence.

Then I thought I would get creative. "Okay, God. What would

you say if I agreed to abstain from sex for one year?" Then, I thought about what I had just said. *No, no, Jakii! You must be crazy to try lying to God!* Next, I continued my prayer from another angle. "Excuse me, God. I know that one year is an unreal stretch for me, so what about six months?" I paused. "How about five months?" I just couldn't lie. "I'll agree to abstain for ninety days!"

I figured that I had already gone that long before and after giving birth, so surely I could tough it out again. When I finished all of this laborious negotiating, suddenly I broke into laughter. It finally hit me! The only person with whom I was attempting to bargain was myself. God had not, nor would He change His plan just for me.

When I saw Mac for a few times after that, I broke my promise to God. I can honestly say that celibacy didn't come easily or quickly for me. Finally I came to understood deep inside my soul that my self-worth before the Lord was more valuable than any sexual thrill. Besides, Jesus had given up His life so I might have a chance to be free from all the pitfalls and the depth of pain from my past.

As I grew in the Lord, I realized I had been selling myself short. Once I discovered sex normally involved enjoyment instead of pain, I realized that I was merely a play toy for the men with whom I'd been intimate, someone they could enjoy while their wives were looking the other way. I repented to God for the years I had wasted, for the spouses I had hurt, and for the pain I had inflicted upon myself as well. I promised I would never consciously seek another relationship with a married man.

But, regardless of my firm conviction, somehow I managed to keep on attracting them! I ended up dating two more married men after this commitment to God and myself, but both of them deceived me by claiming they were single. They wore no rings and both of them even asked me to marry them.

Only one guy actually gave me an engagement ring, but a year later I discovered he had never signed his final divorce papers. It's hard to believe, but he became very angry and stopped speaking to me when I discovered the truth about him. I saw how easily this type of man can twist his own conscience. Nevertheless, I was the one who had actually been betrayed.

Out of all of this, I did learn an important lesson about how to conduct my life before the Lord. In order to avoid the problem from occurring again, I decided I wouldn't even talk to a married man unless his wife was with him. If a man did approach me, I would ask him directly about his marital status. If he ended up being married, I wouldn't stay around unless the conversation had something to do with business. If a longer talk became necessary, I would ask him to bring his wife over to finish the talk with me. I was delivered, and I was going to make sure I stayed that way.

Chapter 16

Refining the Walk

Hayward, California. . . 1974

As I continued to study the Word of God, I made it a point to attend a good teaching church no matter where my sons and I lived. In Los Angeles I had been working with a finance company, but eventually a savings-and-loan firm asked me to join them in northern California. We relocated to a little town called Foster City about forty minutes south of San Francisco and a fifteen-minute drive from Oakland.

In the mid-1970s, when my youngest son, Scott, was four years old, he was diagnosed with asthma. He was allergic to almost everything in his daily life, including food, and because of his medications, he suffered from headaches twenty-four hours a day for months at a time.

I had to care for Scott most of the day, so I decided to leave the rigid schedule of the corporate world. It was a great financial risk, but I enrolled in cosmetology school because I knew a career in that field would offer a more flexible schedule. I was assured that if I was skilled, I could really make some good money. I graduated in 1977 and went to work in my first salon.

One year later a female client named Linda came in and requested to have me work on her. She claimed that she was thrilled with the way I styled her hair, and she sent me flowers in gratitude. Gifts were not uncommon, so I thought nothing of it. However, it wasn't long before Linda began calling and asking me to join her for a drink. I always refused, but she never failed to keep inviting me.

Linda also found out I was a Christian and wanted to know where I went to church. Her next appeal was to ask me to begin a personal Bible study with her. In the spiritual realm, this seemed to be a good thing, but her requests did not stop there. After we began meeting together for study, she wasted no time in asking me to go out with her.

I had met some of her other Christian friends when she invited me to join them at a birthday celebration, but I was shocked to discover they frequented gay bars and clubs. I had never seen any places like these back in Pittsburgh because Dorothy mostly partied with her lovers and a lot of straight people at regular bars. At least, these were the kinds of people she brought over to the house, and the nightclubs where she worked catered to everyone.

When I returned home that night, I resolved that I could no longer have anything to do with Linda. My plan was to cancel all her Bible studies and hair appointments and make it clear that I didn't want to pursue our friendship. A negative reaction was predictable, but her actual response stopped me in my tracks.

"You know I can make your life a living hell," she announced. "I always get what I want!"

I bravely walked away from her threats, but it was clear she meant what she said. Soon I began getting irate phone calls from her at the salon every day, and somehow she acquired the back room number which was only used for private calls and family emergencies. Once I picked up the phone at work and she announced, "Since you won't see me anymore, I'm going to call your salon manager and tell her, and everyone else in the salon, that you and I are dating. And I'm going to tell your children that we're lovers!"

I slammed the receiver down so hard I thought I had broken the phone. Actually, I had intended to break her eardrum. That was Miss Hyde's reaction, but for days I had been in prayer, asking the Lord to give me a perfect opportunity to talk with my manager. After this phone call, I knew it would be better for everyone to think of me as gay rather than having to spend time with Linda to try to appease her. If the staff somehow refused to believe me, at least in my profession being gay would only enhance my business, not kill it. Therefore, I determined to trust God and tell my manager and my children exactly what was going on with her.

Later that day, when things quieted down in the salon, I took the plunge, pulled my manager aside and told her what was going on. She looked at me and laughed, then called a few of the other co-workers over and told them the big news. To my surprise, they all laughed together. Personally, I failed to see any humor in the situation.

After everyone in the shop composed themselves, my manager turned to me with words of comfort. "Don't worry, Jakii. We know what Linda is about and we won't allow her back here again. We'll make sure all your calls are screened, so don't you even give her another thought."

I stood there in total amazement! I could not believe these people. First of all, they believed me, and secondly, they were willing to stand with me in this problem. I thanked them all profusely and made plans for my next step. I had to tell my children.

The next day I left work early, picked up my sons and we went for a drive. I told them that I had something important to say. I explained about my problem with Linda and what she planned to tell them. My youngest son, Scott, really didn't comprehend, but Durksen sat quietly and listened. When I finished he looked at me and said, "It's okay, Mom, I love you. Can we get some ice cream now?"

As I drove home, I remember talking to God. I thanked Him for all the blessings He had given me in the process of resolving this problem, and then I was struck with another thought. "I have been a good mother to these boys. Each and every day I've been there for them, and because of experiencing God's love in my own life, I've truly learned to love them. If the things Linda wanted to say about me had been true, what right would my sons have to judge me?"

I know lots of people who would not buy the fact that God had really spoken to me. Also, I still know many people who don't believe in the power of the Holy Spirit, but no one could ever challenge what happened next in that car. I heard a Voice just as clear as a bell say to me, "Then what right did you have to judge your mother? Just as you will always be their mother, Dorothy will always be your mother."

It was profound! All my adult life I constantly recited my mother's blatant sins to God. I even added other things I knew or thought she had done wrong. The Lord let me know that day, in no uncertain terms, just how much of a hypocrite I was!

Dorothy was God's creation and He was the only one who had a right to judge her. According to the Bible, we are to honor our mother and father (Ephesians 6:2). It doesn't say we are to wait until they are perfect to honor them. If I was truly a believer in the Most High God, I had to allow Him to deal with my mother. This was not the first time the Holy Spirit had been dealing with me on this very issue.

A few years earlier I had been praying in my bedroom and was asking the Lord to teach me to love Him. I felt directed to look up I John 4:20 where Jesus was asking His followers how they could say they loved Him and still hate their brother. After I read the verse a few times I said, "Lord, I don't hate my brothers."

His reply in the Spirit was, "No, you hate the lady who brought you into this world. You cannot hate her and honestly think you can love Me."

I was floored! I asked God to forgive me, but then I remembered Matthew 5:23-24 which says, "So when you are offering your gift at the altar, if you remember that your brother or sister has something against you, leave your gift there before the altar and go; first be reconciled to your brother or sister, and then come and offer your gift." (RSV) *Does this mean before I can truly love Jesus, I have to forgive Dorothy?* I wondered.

Immediately I picked up the phone and called her. I asked her to forgive me for hating her and being angry with her for so many years. She indicated she had been hurt and confused by my anger, but this time I didn't bring up her shortcomings. Regardless of her response, I simply had to ask for her forgiveness.

Now, in the car with my two sons, the Lord was telling me not to judge her. Whether Dorothy had been right or wrong, I had no right to judge her and keep her imprisoned. I couldn't wait to get on my knees and ask God's forgiveness for my shallow, selfish ways.

That night I phoned Dorothy again and asked her to forgive me for presuming to judge her lifestyle. I meant every word that

I said from the bottom of my heart. Once again, there wasn't much of a response on her part, but I prayed an inner healing would begin to take place within Dorothy's spirit and in my heart.

Remarkably, my client Linda never told anyone the lies she had promised to spread about me. Through this entire situation, God obviously used Linda to help crack my stony heart. When I let Dorothy off the hook by not being her judge, I was also helping myself out of bondage and into freedom. I was discovering my walk with Jesus was going to be a real adventure. With each new step came the pain of revelation about my self, but then came the joy, hope and healing. *How much more work does the Lord have to do within me?* I wondered.

Chapter 17

Moving Forward

By 1984 I had been saved for eleven years, and for the most part, my life involved taking care of Scott, teaching two weekly Bible studies at Hayward Bible Chapel, and doing hair and make-up in salons, as well as for television commercials, infomercials and music videos. My oldest son had already graduated from high school, and after spending six months in a junior college, he decided to enlist in the military. I prayed that I had done enough as a single parent, with the Lord's help, to send him out into the world on his own.

Another major milestone in my life at that time was the fact that I finally repented of lying to all my pastors. Unfortunately, I had lied about Dorothy. Originally I had told them my mother was dead, even though she was still alive. I even had to repent to my sons, especially Scott because that summer I was planning to take him back to Pittsburgh to visit my family. I certainly didn't want him to be surprised when I introduced him to the grandmother he thought was dead!

This trip was also crucial for me because I was determined to spend some time with Dorothy, and I was hopeful my phone calls had softened her a bit. I arranged the trip so we would spend one week with my brother and the next week with my father's family. In order to visit him, we were going to stay with Cleophas' youngest sister and her family.

During our first night in town, "Uncle" Bobby brought Dorothy and Uncle Charles to see us at Reggie's house. In the sixteen years Reggie had been married, Dorothy had never visited his home, although she only lived twenty minutes by car from their place. It was hard not to add this to my list of criticisms, but I wanted somehow to see her in a new light.

That night we all sat around talking and laughing for at least two hours. Dorothy seemed to feel at ease because she was in her comfort zone with Uncle Charles and "Uncle" Bobby by her side, but I noticed she didn't direct any of her conversation towards me. My brother came up with the idea of having a picnic that week so we could visit with as many family members as possible. Everyone was enthusiastic, but Dorothy mentioned she would have to check her schedule. True to form, she called a day later and informed me she had to go out of town to visit one of her "friends."

Even though my son and I had traveled thousands of miles to be there, and this would have been another chance to spend time with both of her children and grandchildren, it appeared she still could not bring herself to let down her cherished lovers. It felt like old times again. Still, my brother and I had a great time together. Reggie had married his high school sweetheart and now had three sons of his own. It was wonderful to see my son bonding with the cousins he had never known, and I had a chance to spend time with my nephews.

When Dorothy returned home the following week, my father's side of the family also decided to give a little backyard barbecue so everyone could get together. I decided to call Reggie and

Dorothy to see if they could join us. My brother showed up, but Dorothy had another excuse. She claimed that she couldn't come because Cleophas was going to be there.

I broke into hysterical laughter. "You two have not been married for over thirty years and now you want to lay this sad story on me?" I challenged her. "You're just being silly and lying about why you don't want to come." I would not let her get away so easily. "Why can't you just be honest? You and Cleophas have been together for several funerals and other gatherings over the years. The truth is that you just don't want to be around your children!"

She had no ready response, and after unloading my feelings, I said good-bye and hung up the phone. Naturally, I was more than disappointed to think my obedience to the Lord had not brought around more of a change in her. There had to be more to the healing process than I was aware of! The two-week visit to Pittsburgh was wonderful in many ways, but I knew God's work with Dorothy and with me was not yet complete.

Later that same year, my youngest son, Scott, became so ill he had to be hospitalized. He was on oxygen twenty-four hours a day except during his breathing treatments. I had to work during the day, but I spent the rest of my waking hours with him at the hospital. By the first Sunday morning of November I was extra tired, my son was having one of his worst asthma attacks, and I felt a strong yearning to go to church. I was really looking forward to a word of comfort from the Lord.

Senior Pastor Jim Matthews always gave the most pertinent messages, but once I arrived, I realized the youth pastor was leading the service. I found myself sitting in the pew pouting. *Why him, Lord?* Obviously, God had not heard my request. I needed a sermon that would comfort this grieving mother's heart. After all, my son was sick and we needed God to do a quick healing in his lungs or he could die.

The youth pastor was preaching from the fifth chapter of Matthew about loving your enemies. He read from the scripture where Jesus says it's not enough to only love those who love us, but we must also love our enemies (Matthew 5:43-44). The pastor looked up from his notes and asked, "Who is your enemy?" and went on to explain. "To me, an enemy is an unlovable person. Who do you have in your life that is unlovable? Tell God who you consider to be an unlovable person in your eyes today."

Obediently, I gave in and thought for a while. *Okay, God! Who is this person who's unlovable to me?*

The name "Sandy" came to mind. My immediate reaction was, *You must be losing it for real, girl!* Sandy was a very nice client of mine. I paused and looked upward. *God, you've really missed it this time if Sandy is the person you just laid upon my heart!*

Inside this small church on that particular Sunday morning, the Lord again met me right there in that pew and did business with my heart. "Jacqueline," He said, "this morning I want to do more than heal your son's lungs, I want to heal your heart."

But how does Sandy fit in with you healing my heart? I wanted to know.

In my spirit the Lord pointed out that Sandy was a lesbian and my heart was full of anger toward lesbians. At this time the term "lesbian" was finally replacing the usual slang terms I had been accustomed to, but the revelation was just too much for me to swallow.

But, Lord, I don't hate Sandy, I mentally responded.

There was silence.

After church, my mind went back to the critical situation at hand. A friend drove me back to the hospital again. Scott didn't want me to leave when my friend was ready to go, so I stayed longer than usual. However, I had no clue how I was going to get home because the buses stopped running after a certain time in the little town of Hayward. It would end up being quite a long walk home from the train station in the dark, so I prayed about the situation and waited for God to open a door.

My answer came quickly, but it didn't come from someone I would have expected or even wanted. Sandy, the client God had pointed out to me in church, telephoned my son's hospital room to see how he was doing. Little did I know that she and her lover had been stopping by the hospital to visit him almost every night because they lived so close to the hospital. When Sandy discovered I was there, she asked if they could take me to dinner. They knew I had been at church and the hospital all day and it was after five in the evening.

I agreed to their offer but I was very uncomfortable. All the craziness I had gone through with Linda was still fresh in my mind, and I had made a rule not to spend free time with any of my clients outside of business hours. Still, my stomach was growling from lack of food, so I decided to break my rule for this one occasion. Besides, Sandy and her friend were being so nice to Scott and I didn't feel right being rude.

When they arrived to pick me up, all I could think about was the fact that I was a hypocrite! I was still thinking about the things the Lord had revealed to me that morning about my own heart and my real feelings about Sandy's lifestyle. By accepting their hospitality, I would be using them to meet my needs without having any real desire to be around them.

Dinner was very nice, but by the time we finished it was getting late. Also, my son had requested that I bring him some of his special milk so he could eat cereal the next morning. He was using Mocha Mix and it was so new the hospital was not offering it yet. I had promised to deliver it before I went home, and now I realized if I purchased the milk, I wouldn't have enough money for the train.

While I was in the back seat of their car thinking about the problem, Sandy suggested they take me to the store to get the milk and then back to the nurses' station at the hospital to deliver it. Unfortunately, we couldn't locate a store that was still open and carried that brand of milk, so Sandy suggested I stay overnight at their house. Then, in the morning before breakfast, she or her friend would take me to the store and then to the hospital to drop the milk off. I was truly shaken with this idea!

The last time I had slept in the same room with two lesbians, I had wakened to the sounds of lovemaking. Regardless of my fears, I knew I had to take Sandy and her friend up on their offer, so I prayed God would let me sleep soundly through the night. Unbelievably, I did! They were so wonderful to me that next morning I felt ashamed of myself. After our mission was completed, Sandy pushed some money in my hand so I could buy a ticket for the train.

God really opened my eyes to my ugly heart and I prayed all the way home and the following week for Him to forgive me and to clean up my heart and life. Sandy and I became very good friends, and a few years later the Lord gave me the pleasure of seeing her go forward in church to accept Jesus Christ into her life!

However, the complete healing God intended for me had only just begun. There was more. Suddenly, the lights came on inside my spirit concerning the connection between Sandy and Dorothy. Until that day, all lesbians were my enemies because they all represented Dorothy and her way of life. She had always put her lovers first, second, and third in her life—leaving no room for my brother or me.

God, in His wisdom, knew if He had revealed Dorothy as my

enemy, I would have blocked out anything He had to show me. Placing someone else before my eyes with whom I didn't have issues was the perfect way to show me the similarity between Sandy and Dorothy. God wanted to heal my anger as well as my critical spirit against Dorothy and her lifestyle.

Once again, I wish I could say my own healing happened overnight, but it didn't. The miracle was that it finally did happen. I had forgiven Dorothy for the way she had treated me as a child and I had asked for forgiveness for judging her as a mother. However, I had never stopped judging her for being a lesbian and for bringing all of her shame on my brother and me.

Because of Dorothy's lifestyle, people always treated me as though I was a leper or some kind of diseased animal. For some reason they thought I was going to pounce upon their children and lead them "into temptation." I was labeled and excluded because people assumed I was like my mother, and I hated Dorothy for that. That was the real reason I decided to pronounce her dead when I moved to California and vowed to never look back.

Now God was telling me it was time to come out of my make-believe world and tell people that Dorothy was alive. That meant I had to confess to all the important people in my life that I had been living a lie. To this date, my pastors and only a few other people knew the truth. Now it would have to become public knowledge for me to walk free of my lies and deception.

"Okay, Lord," I responded, "I'll reveal my deep secret, but you know I'm going to be labeled again and shut out again. Do you really think your saved people are any different from unsaved ones when it comes to the subject of prejudice?"

"Let me worry about that," I heard in my heart. "You just tell the truth."

You should have seen the look on some of the faces when I

told my friends and co-workers about my mother and the fact she was alive. I saw a lot of dental work when their mouths fell open and they shook their heads in disbelief.

God was just preparing me because the following year—1985—my pastors invited me to attend a meeting where the leaders of the church were coming together to discuss how they should move forward in evangelism. I had been teaching Bible classes and had earned their respect, and I knew it was an honor to be invited to their insiders' meeting. God laid it on my heart to announce that the church needed to be ready to witness to gay men and women who would give their lives to Jesus Christ and would desire to step out of homosexuality.

I remember asking God at that time, "Is it really possible? Can people really walk away from the gay lifestyle and be changed and happy?"

This time I didn't hear anything, but I did remember a verse in Jeremiah where God poses the question, "Is anything too hard for me?" (Jeremiah 32:27)

I knew the answer to that question was "No!" Anything that God made, He certainly would know how to change or help. He created man in His own image, so He knows how to help man and has the exact tools to use effectively. All that man needs to do is to be willing.

In my presentation to the leaders, I explained how we needed to reach people from the homosexual community who had given their lives to Jesus Christ. In order to do so, we needed to understand their unique pain and hurts. These individuals would need special assistance to help them through their transition time because they would most likely end up leaving their lovers and a whole lot of friends. In fact, their whole lifestyle would be changing. It would take people who were trained and compassionate to help them.

I was not prepared for the church leaders' general response: "We're not ready to have 'them' in our church!" My heart stopped in my chest and disappointment flooded my soul.

That night I realized something I had never considered. If Dorothy were to get saved and come to live with me, these same people who hugged me every Sunday and sat through my classes would probably not want to receive Dorothy into their homes.

This same night I also discovered God had really done a healing in my own heart toward my mother. I realized that I would now be able to allow her into my home, and it grieved my heart to think that my brothers and sisters in Christ, with whom I had broken bread for eleven years, would not be willing to help disciple her. Still, with all the work the Lord had done in my life, I knew there was more deliverance waiting for me.

Chapter 18

About Miss Hyde

During the 1984-1985 school year I signed up for a twelve-unit counseling course taught by a Christian psychologist. It was designed for graduate students, but if the students were not interested in receiving the degree, they could still read all the books and turn in the same reports. If they ended up passing the final exams, they could apply for a Lay Counselor's Certificate. The other option was for students to take the course as an observer. Since I was not a graduate candidate, I opted for the Lay Counselor's Certificate.

At the end of the first quarter I handed in all of the homework required for a grade, but during the second quarter I changed my mind. Now I only wanted to be an observer and I didn't hand in any of the homework for the second or third quarters. Work had been hectic and I thought that I'd just glean information for myself. During the fourth quarter, there was a special presentation on child abuse which stopped me in my tracks.

As I listened that evening, I had such a feeling of empathy for the speaker. She was a doctor of psychology and a survivor of child abuse, so she spoke from book knowledge as well as personal experience. She listed several characteristics of an abused child. Five of them hit me right between my eyes and I couldn't have missed them if I had been blind.

First she explained the "bully spirit." According to her, abused children would go one of two ways. They would end up taking on the characteristics of a bully or those of a "doormat." As I wondered about myself, I knew I had consistently shut down many painful experiences and memories. But then I thought back to what my brother Reggie used to say. As an adult he chuckled when he confessed he would run to find me whenever someone threatened to hurt him because he knew I would beat them up!

I always found this hard to believe about myself when I heard these reports because I was thoroughly convinced I was a wimp. However, I found myself doubting my "doormat" feelings when I reflected on my fights with Kemp. I used to get quite physical when I'd had enough of his running around or when he tried to make me feel inferior.

I realized that I was not a "doormat" type of personality; this type of person would never have stood up to Dorothy. When I was twelve years old I had the audacity to threaten her life. When I thought about it further, I always assumed it was Miss Hyde who defended me and I was not responsible for her actions. She was my protector, but now I had to face the truth: I had a "bully spirit."

The psychologist went on to explain the attributes of a caretaker, another characteristic of an abused child. This person had the constant need to care for someone else before taking care of herself. I must admit, when Reggie was first born I didn't like him. He cried all the time and I had to wash his smelly diapers. Then one day Dorothy came home in a particularly foul mood and began to yell at him. At that point I made up my mind to watch over him and I found myself actually loving the little brat.

So, at nine years old, I decided not to let Dorothy abuse him the way she had hurt me. In that sense, I had taken on the responsibilities of a mother figure even before I was in the fifth grade. Of course, I took care of him from the moment Dorothy left him, but I was doing it purely out of duty that first year. Grandmere was the only person who ever looked after me, but when we were away from her protection, Dorothy would treat me worse than ever. Because I didn't want this to happen to Reggie, I was determined to do the best I could for my brother. I became the caretaker, and of course we had to be together all the time. As far as babies go, I realize now that he wasn't so bad. However, it wasn't good for a nine-year-old child to have a "caretaker spirit."

When the psychologist mentioned that abused children often had problems with low self-esteem, I didn't have to ponder that one! She said they either developed this quality, or became very arrogant and prideful. Both were cover-ups for pain. I knew I didn't like the inner Jakii very much, and low-self esteem was practically my middle name.

Of course, I could dress the part on the outside: I had very good manners, proper speech, and I knew which fork to use. But inside I felt worthless. I had only dated married men before I found the Lord because I hadn't felt that I deserved a real man of my own. I never really understood why I felt this way, but I would laugh and pretend that everything was great while others were around. When I was alone, I would cry. After listening to the psychologist's talk, I felt there might be hope for me.

The doctor also explained that being an overachiever meant the person never liked coming second in anything. I wondered why this was on the list of possible problems an abused child would face, but I definitely couldn't deny this one, either. I had always been very competitive and enjoyed a challenge.

Finally, the most hard-hitting of all the characteristics of abused children was the development of a second or third personality to survive the trauma. Could this explain the identity of my very own protectorate, Miss Hyde? I sat in class remembering that morning at 200 South Euclid when Dorothy first threatened to beat me. The conversation I had with Miss Hyde was as if another person were speaking to me. I didn't feel any of the blows Dorothy delivered to my body, and now realized I had truly learned to separate myself from what was actually happening to me.

To be perfectly honest, Miss Hyde was no real surprise when she showed up the day of the beating. I must have known her from before, but at this point my memory didn't go back that far. Maybe there had been other instances prior to that horrible occasion when she had first appeared to me. I was going to have to think about that one.

I also recalled a time when I stood up in a chair and told a six-foot-three inch man I would kill him if he ever hurt me again, and I meant it! Other outlandish things I was responsible for were told to me when I was older, but they had never surfaced in my own memory. Because so many people had repeated these same stories to me over the years, I knew they must have been true.

After the lecture, the class separated into assigned groups so we could talk about the new information. On other occasions, I was one of the first to let my thoughts be known, but this night was different. Instead, I listened to the group members who claimed they had heard about or knew someone who had been molested. They were talking about fathers, brothers, cousins and other family members who had committed the abuse.

During the discussion, someone in the room mentioned the

phrase "foster father." Suddenly all my strength was gone and I could hardly keep from breaking down in tears. I really had no idea why I wanted to cry, but I felt as though elephants were sitting on my chest. *Perhaps, I thought, I am just grieving for the psychologist and the pain she personally suffered.*

I didn't speak a word during the entire class, and as soon as I entered my house that night, I went upstairs to the bathroom. I sat down on the side of the bathtub and tried to remember the men who were in my life before I was five years old. Now that I thought about it again, I was sure Miss Hyde was not new to me when I moved into the Edward's household.

Something horrible had definitely happened to me as a foster child. I hated to think about it because I had loved the Williams so much, but the Holy Spirit was pressing in on me.

The first person I thought of was my foster father's brother. I called him "Unkie" since I could never say the proper pronunciation. The name stuck with him, but as I thought about my memories of him, nothing happened. I had no tears or reaction.

My father, Cleophas, came to my mind as well. Other than the short week he and Dorothy lived together at Grandmere's home, I only remembered him coming to visit me once or twice as a small child when he was wearing a white navy uniform. I drew a blank, so I kept on probing my past.

The third person I considered was my foster father, Thomas Williams. This time, as soon as I said his name, I burst into uncontrollable tears. I curled up into a ball on the bathroom rug and cried for at least twenty minutes. I couldn't stop the flow as hard as I tried. When finally I pulled myself together, I went to the telephone to call my pastor's father who was a licensed counselor.

I was shocked at his words. "Jakii, I've known for years you have some deep abuse issues, but since you refused to talk about anything, I could never help you."

Had I really been that defensive? Did other people see this denial in me as well? I wondered.

"Please," he begged me, "don't let this moment pass without making an appointment to see a counselor!" Before I hung up, he made me promise to seek further counseling.

I scheduled an appointment the next day, and when I arrived I had already convinced myself that it was all in my mind. Most likely I had just flipped out over the stories the lecturer told us about her own abuse issues. In my first session I told the counselor I had made a mistake and really didn't need to see him, but one session led to many others.

Finally, we worked through to the point when I had to admit what I felt the night I was sexually abused by the only father figure I knew at that young age. I also learned that I really had created an alter personality to cope during that incomprehensible trauma. Facing the entire incident was like standing naked at twelve noon in the middle of Wilshire Boulevard in Beverly Hills. I was totally exposed and uncovered. That was an extremely hard day for me.

My imagination hadn't been working overtime, and finally I came face-to-face with the truth about my past. God had graciously led me to this particular place for counseling so I could be set free, and I ended up choosing to forgive Daddy Williams and love him, even though he had already been dead for many years. I also realized why Miss Hyde came into my life at such an early age.

As long as Miss Hyde was at my side, I didn't have to feel any pain while the bad events were happening. As I had already discovered, sometimes I would completely forget incidents and other people would tell me about them. At other times, the memories would come back as short, very quick dreams. They ·

were similar to *déjà vu* type situations when you think you know something but you can't put your finger on the details.

While I worked through my series of counseling sessions, I also continued with the classes at the counseling center. By now I had decided to become a lay counselor but I had to finish reading all of the books required on the second and third quarters' reading list, and submit a written report on them. In the fourth quarter I also submitted my self-evaluation paper. I am pleased to say that I received one of the top grades in my group and was also awarded my coveted counselor's certificate. Hopefully, I would be better equipped to face up to any new revelations that would sneak up and rock me from time to time.

Chapter 19

From Dorothy to Mother

Early in July 1987, I made another trip back to Pittsburgh for my high school reunion. During this otherwise uneventful trip, I made an important breakthrough with Dorothy. At this point she was living with her sister Ruthie and for the first time in my life I hugged her and told her I loved her. Once again, I had no idea how she was affected because there wasn't much of a reply, but it was a red-letter event for me.

During the same year I joined Jubilee Christian Center in San Jose, California, and I began asking God if He would change my finances so I could bring Dorothy out to California to care for her. She was showing signs of Alzheimer's disease and eventually she would have to be placed in a nursing home and then a convalescent hospital.

In 1989, I was teaching a women's Bible study from the book of James. It had to do with mercy, and James explained if judgment is what you give, judgment is what you will receive. If you give mercy, mercy is what you will receive (James 2:13). To illustrate, I gave the class a brief background on my relationship with Dorothy. I also shared that while I was preparing for the lesson, the Holy Spirit had pointed out something to me. Even though I had forgiven my mother and stopped judging her lifestyle, now I needed to go a step further and grant her mercy.

I went on to explain, "Judgment means you have done something wrong and have been found guilty. The person who judges you then withholds their friendship or love. Mercy, on the other hand, means that you have indeed done something wrong, but instead of being punished, that person who was wronged is going to forgive you and continue to be your friend. With God's influence they could even go on to love and pray for you. That is mercy! In other words, judgment gives a person what they deserve, while mercy holds back what they deserve and lets them off the hook."

Everyone in the class seemed to be with me. The ladies heard how I had come to love my mother with a love that was deeper than anything I could have ever hoped for. This new love meant that now I wanted to care for the woman who had supposedly hated me all her life. God had taught me to love her unconditionally. This had not happened because she changed toward me, but because God had changed my heart with His love. I could honestly tell these women that finally I could call Dorothy "mother" with a pure heart and I truly did love her.

I deeply regretted all the years I had spent hating her when I could have stepped out in faith with love and forgiveness and developed some kind of relationship with her. When I finished with the lesson, most of the women came forward to seek forgiveness for the years of hate and anger they had harbored against various people in their lives, many who had anger toward their mothers. It was pure joy for me to know God was allowing me to use my mistakes and growth in His Word to reach out and help others.

God had already placed within me a vision for ministering to homosexuals in 1985, and the rejection from that church still stung within me. However, in September 1990 the Lord spoke to me about it again. This time He prompted me to offer the same program to Pastor Dick Bernal at Jubilee Christian Center. I was to form a support/recovery group to help brothers and sisters who wanted to leave homosexuality. I knew that many of these people would never be able to tell any other Christian about their past without being judged and shut out. It could also help people like me who had been raised in a homosexual environment. I definitely thought this type of program would be valuable at this huge church in such a strategic location in the San Francisco Bay Area, but I remained quiet because I didn't want to be rejected again. But of course I made my feelings clear to God!

In early October 1990, I heard the Lord give me the same message again. I was to talk to Pastor Bernal. "He's too busy to see me," I told God.

On Halloween, Pastor Bernal was appearing on a television talk show about deliverance and healing. As I sat in the audience at the church watching the program with the rest of the staff, I heard a voice call out my name.

"Jacqueline."

I turned around and there was no one close enough to be talking to me. I went back to watching the screen.

"Jacqueline."

When I looked around again and saw no one, I knew it had to be the voice of God, so I answered, "Here I am, Father."

"I told you to give that program to Pastor Bernal. He's going to need it."

"But, if I do that, everyone will think I'm gay! And besides, they don't want this plan any more than the other church did." I sounded like a grumbling Old Testament Israelite.

Again I heard the voice, "I told you to give the plan to him."

This time I didn't argue. "Yes, Sir!" I said.

As soon as the program was over I headed straight to the pastor's office to make an appointment with his secretary. I had to meet with him as soon as possible and I wasted no time in making preparations for our meeting. I came up with a short outline of things I should consider when proposing the ministry:

A. Who were the people I was targeting to come?

B. Why did I think we needed such a ministry?

C. What did I hope to accomplish through the ministry?

D. How would I find these people?

As I walked into the pastor's office the day of our meeting, my knees were trembling. His desk seemed more massive than I had remembered and he seemed like a giant towering over me. I took my chair and handed him my plan. As he looked it over, I watched while holding my breath. Then, he pivoted his chair in my direction and looked directly into my eyes. "Why are you qualified to lead such a group?" he asked.

I wanted to jump out of my skin and run from the room, but the only thing that kept me in my seat was the knowledge that God would send me back again if I failed to follow through.

"Well. . . ," I stammered, "I've been teaching Bible studies for almost seventeen years now and I was raised by a lesbian mother. Outside of the fact that I know God has called me to this ministry, I guess nothing else really qualifies me. You can be sure I'd never think this up all by myself!"

Pastor Bernal tried to hide a grin, probably aware that I was really nervous. He asked me a few more questions and then told me something so profound that I have never forgotten it.

"You know, Jakii, a lot of those people you know and think are your friends—you know, the ones who hug you after the service and pat you on the back about the great lesson you taught—won't even want to sit next to you in church after you begin this ministry." I knew exactly what he was talking about. "They certainly won't hug you in public where others can see them. Are you prepared for that?"

I didn't hesitate. "Yes, I believe I am. I've been shunned most of my life because of my mother's lifestyle, so I think I'm an expert on being shut out." In retrospect, I must have sounded a lot like Peter when Jesus was trying to tell him Satan had asked to sift him like wheat (Luke 22:31). Peter's modern-day response would have been something like, "No problem, Jesus, I think I can handle it!"

After further discussion, Pastor Bernal said he would pray about the ministry and get back to me. The next week I left for a trip to Atlanta, and I was rather relieved that I didn't have to worry about the ministry at this point. I had been obedient, but in my heart I was sure Pastor Bernal would turn the idea down just as the other church had done.

It wasn't long before I received a call from the assistant of the associate pastor telling me that the project had been approved and that Pastor wanted to know when I would be able to start setting up the ministry. I was amazed at the miracle God had pulled off! It had to be God and God alone who had opened that ministry "for such a time as this" (Esther 4:14).

While I was still in Atlanta I wrote the lesson plans for the ministry and set up its parameters. Once I returned to California I rounded up a stack of books to read every day so I could learn as much as I could about the hurts, pains, joys and struggles of the men and women who were caught in homosexuality. As I continued my research, I received the most incredible revelation that homosexuals had many of the same issues that I did. I displayed my pain through relationships with married men, and homosexuals accomplished the same thing with their same-sex partners. I named the fledgling ministry "New Beginnings," because that is what I felt abused people needed.

There was no publicity, just an announcement from the pulpit for our first meeting in 1991, and over thirty-five people showed up. Some even came from other churches. The need was great, and I knew the Lord would give me the strength and wisdom to lead this ministry. Still, I had no idea of all that was in store for me.

Once the ministry began, I found myself working one-on-one with born-again men and women who still struggled with homosexual behavior. After a while I found myself facing the old fears I thought were behind me. All throughout my twenties, thirties and into my forties, I lived with the fear that one day I might wake up and discover I was a lesbian.

I began asking myself, "Am I sexually attracted to women?" The answer was "No." So why was I afraid? I was still remembering all the things people had said about me in the past. These statements were not based upon who I was, but solely upon the reputation of my mother.

Some days it was like having a hand pushing me in the back and saying, "You might as well kill yourself because you know you're gay!" For several months, every day became a battle. My inner conflict didn't involve seeking a female lover; my battle was whether or not I should live out the day or kill myself! Obviously, the ministry was taking a toll on me.

So many times I asked God why I was being tormented. The answer came to me in a powerful revelation. Satan had an assignment against my life and he was using doubts, fears and inner vows I had carried all of those years to wear me down. He didn't want me working in a ministry where I was helping people find a new way of living.

One day when the battle was particularly intense, I remembered John 3:16 which promised that God had given His only Son for my deliverance. All I had to do was accept His gift. If I was to have deliverance, I had to know what was stopping me from receiving it. "God, I have received Jesus as my Savior, and I have lived pretty much free of these thoughts for so many years. Why are they coming back now?"

Then the verses from I John 1:8-9 came to me. I had to confess my sins so I could be forgiven and cleansed of them.

"What sins have I failed to confess?" I asked. "I'm not trying to live the homosexual lifestyle and I'm not looking for a woman. So, what am I missing? What am I failing to see?"

The Holy Spirit responded with one word: "Fear."

Immediately I realized that coping with constant fear was a living death, and I repented for carrying that spirit of fear. My firm decision that day was that fear would no longer rule my life. If I was going to be gay, then at least I knew that I could turn my sins over to Jesus and He had the power to forgive me and make me whole. The moment I faced my fear, that stronghold broke and I have never been afraid of becoming a lesbian again. But to this day, I must stay on guard against the spirit of fear because it can and does rear its ugly head in so many areas of one's life.

With this new spiritual understanding, all the pressure lifted from me. I did run across someone later who did not understand the call of God on my life. She constantly told me that I should watch myself because she "just knew" that I had a tendency to be drawn into the spirit of lesbianism.

From her point of view, she was correct because I had been raised by a woman who lived that lifestyle, and according to her,

I was simply in hiding from my deepest desires. She thought that I should get out of this type of ministry. But I knew with certainty I was called to minister to men and women who wanted out of the homosexual life and to help with their healing process. God had given to me love for the men and women whom I once hated because I viewed them all as Dorothy. I could identify with their wounds, hurts, and years of low self-esteem. I could also minister to the children of homosexuals, and there were more of them than I had ever considered.

I dedicated my ministry to Dorothy and often wondered what the circumstances were that locked her into lesbianism. I knew she had an uncle on R.G.'s side who had been quite a notorious "queen" in his time even though I could hardly remember him. It became clear to me, as I studied my own family, that children who have homosexuals in their family often have gender identity problems, especially if they are close to that gay person.

If these children somehow managed to dodge the lure of homosexuality, they still had to deal with the same inner conflicts I had taken so long to overcome. Abused children tend to follow many of the same patterns of behavior and mental anguish when they became parents.

For example, I had learned in my psychology classes that the learned traits of violence and rape had been known to pass down though generations of victims. My own family had been the perfect example. The more I counseled, the clearer these patterns emerged.

In 1992 I moved from Hayward to San Jose to be closer to my church, and as I continued to minister to others, my heart kept turning back to my mother in Pittsburgh. I knew there was no one there who could talk with her and no classes were available to help her work through her own issues. I also knew that Dorothy was not looking for any help. To the best of my knowledge, she lived the life of a lesbian until Alzheimer's incapacitated her. But, in my spirit, I knew the Lord was calling me to minister to as many people as possible who were just like her.

At the same time, I began asking God to send a witness to my mother to tell her about the saving grace of Jesus Christ. I knew the disease was destroying her brain, but God had created the brain, and if anyone knew how to get truth to her, who could do it better than the One who created her? I also asked God to examine my heart and to search me through and through to see if there were any wicked ways left in me regarding my mother and the life she had led. If God had healed me, why would He want my mother to suffer any longer?

Dorothy had recently lost both her feet to gangrene due to the untreated bed sores she suffered while staying at the facility. I certainly didn't want to see these people continue to cut her up because she had stopped walking. Eventually her body, I was told, would begin to malfunction and I didn't want her to suffer. Mostly, I wanted to be sure my mother received Jesus Christ as her Lord and Savior so one day we could have the relationship in glory that we were never able to have here on earth. I kept my prayers before the throne room of God and found peace knowing she was in His hands.

On April 8, 1992, my brother Reggie called to tell me our mother had died. She had not suffered a heart attack or had renal failure. She simply went to sleep. In faith I believed my prayers had been answered, and so I quietly sat down and wrote a prayer about my mom: "Lord, this comes from your prodigal daughter who has come back to her roots to join with you, Jehovah, and all the host of heaven in welcoming home your child and my mother, Dorothy Edwards Wright. She's now in the presence of her King.

"I know you could have given me another mother who had it

all together, but Dorothy was your divine choice for me. Father, thank you for my mother, Dorothy. Thank you for allowing me to have Dorothy in my life, and forgive me for not doing all that I could to spend more time with her. I know my mother and I will have a wonderful time in glory together and I know it will bless her to see what you will do with my life and our relationship. I love you, my God, and I love you, Dorothy!"

After my mother's death, I had a new confidence that God would continue working His plan through me. Even if I had to face more pain concerning my past in order to be completely set free and help others, I knew Jesus would teach me.

Chapter 20

The Death of Miss Hyde

From San Jose, California to Atlanta, Georgia . . . 1993 - present

New Beginnings was a successful ministry, and in 1993, I was invited by the Christian Broadcasting Network to appear on their program, "The 700 Club." The producers asked me to talk about my testimony and the experiences I was having in helping people find their way out of homosexuality.

The day before I left for Virginia Beach, I was on my way to get my nails done. This may seem rather vain, but I had worked with video companies doing hair and make-up for the filming of commercials, and I knew the cameras often zoomed in close. I wanted everything about me to be presentable!

As I approached a traffic light near the salon, a car crossed over three lanes to jump in front of me. I blew my horn as the man slammed on his breaks at the light. Then, he purposefully let his car roll back to the point where he crunched up against my bumper. I couldn't move because of the heavy traffic behind me, but he got out to examine the damage he had done to his own car. He refused to look at me and was oblivious to the fact that I was the recipient of his rash act.

"Hey, what's your problem?" I yelled as I leaned out my window.

He never said a word. Instead, he got back into his car, pulled it forward, and then proceeded to call me all sorts of names over a loud speaker installed in his car. By this time I was really upset. Even though I was a "saved, Spirit-filled Christian woman," I was not going to let him get the best of me!

He kept calling me names, and the next thing I knew, I was out of my car trying to pull his head through the window of his car. At the same time, he was desperately trying to roll his window up to save himself! It was difficult for the guy because my fist was poised to punch him in the face. However, his other hand was still on his microphone and he continued to bad-mouth me to the passengers in the nearby cars. We created quite a scene!

Somewhere in my fog of anger, the Holy Spirit allowed me to listen to the things this guy was saying about me. Then I heard the Holy Spirit: "Look at what you're doing. You're acting just like the names he's calling you!" The Holy Spirit also pointed out that this was actually Miss Hyde acting up, and her spirit was nothing but pure anger. "She has to die," I heard God's voice instructing me.

She was pure anger? I paused to let the concept sink in. I never knew that about her and I explained to the Lord that I always thought she was my protector.

"But I am your shield and buckler. I am your very present help in time of trouble. You need to learn to trust Me with your problems," I heard the Lord speaking to me. I had never considered Miss Hyde in this light, and if what I had heard was truly from the Lord, then I had no choice but to give her up.

Once the long-awaited green light allowed the incident to dissipate, I repented for my angry spirit. "Lord, I don't know how to get rid of Miss Hyde, but I'm willing if you will show me how," I promised.

The "how" ended up being a process of stopping at each hurtful, resentful issue and taking the time to pray over it. The answer was to give the person or incident over to Jesus and allow Him to take care of the situation. I also had to go one step further and forgive the people who had hurt me. I would never be allowed to hold grudges against them again. On the other side of the coin, I also had to ask the Lord to forgive me for the often brutal things I had done to others. I was sure there were more incidents than I could ever remember.

In each new situation I had to seek the Holy Spirit's wisdom as to how to deal with other people, and I learned to walk away, pray for them, and allow the Lord to do the healing in my heart. I even had to forgive the man whose face I wanted to rearrange. It seems funny now, but the next time he saw me on that same street, he quickly crossed over three lanes of traffic in front of me. However, this time he was doing it to stay away from me!

I do not see Miss Hyde now, but I had to acknowledge that it is okay for me to be angry with someone without allowing my old protectorate to help out. I no longer need Miss Hyde to take care of my difficulties because now I now know the Lord is my problem-solver.

I did appear as a guest on "The 700 Club" with co-host Terry Meussen, and it turned out very well. Still, I had to laugh as I prepared for my interview, just thinking that a day earlier my ungodly side had been out making a scene.

Although this unique ministry received media attention and the Lord did a tremendous work, after four years of service I was ready to retire. I was exhausted, dissatisfied with my day job, and just wanted to be able to attend church and sit through other people's Bible study classes. The Lord wanted to do more work within me and I was ready.

After deep prayer and consideration, in 1996 I resigned my membership at Jubilee Christian Center and moved to Atlanta, Georgia. Initially I stayed with some wonderful Christian friends, and it wasn't long before I discovered World Changers Church International (WCCI) in nearby College Park. It was awesome! From November 1996 until May 1998, all I did was attend services, listen and read the Bible.

I knew God was calling me to return to the support/recovery ministry but I found myself fighting against it. Thankfully, the church required all new members to attend special classes before anyone could serve in a ministry. This bought me some time, but after completion everyone was encouraged to participate in the ministries of their choice.

When it was my turn to select, first I signed up for everything but the Overcomer's Ministry, which is WCCI's support/recovery group. However, no one would take me into their ministry teams. There were various reasons, but basically none of them were right for me. Then, when I finally talked to Kowalsky, the acting director at that time of the support/recovery ministry, I honestly thought he was a nut case. This made me certain I didn't want to serve in that particular ministry.

Eventually I quit resisting my calling and joined the ministry where Kowalsky and a woman named Pam were the leaders. Kowalsky and I grew to like each other and the three of us became like a family. I began teaching again and now have had the privilege of developing training materials as well. It has ended up being a tremendous blessing to serve with them.

When I minister to others who have been raised by homosexuals, or ex-gay men and women, I remember to address all the areas I had to deal with myself over the long years of recovery:

Years of anger and the alter-personality designed to help me cope covered up many behavior problems I was never even aware of.

There were years of self-doubt, which tormented me, and the put-downs from other people only confirmed my pain and doubt.

I had serious doubts regarding my own sexuality and feared one day I would wake up a lesbian like my mother.

I wondered if people could really love me for who I was because I carried a deep root of shame.

Years of my life were actually blocked out and I was left with little or no memory of many events. My brother recalls things that I cannot remember because I used to shut down as a way to survive the hurt and pain of not being wanted.

Most of my adult life, I had felt like the third head of a two-headed person. I was a total misfit and never felt I belonged with anyone.

Groups of people always made me feel uncomfortable because I thought they were simply tolerating me and were not sincere about wanting me to be with them.

I had a very hard time believing a man could honestly love me because Dorothy didn't love me. Sometimes I even doubted that God really loved me when I did not hear or could not hear from Him.

Love was a difficult concept for me to understand and express. I loved my sons with all my heart, but I never knew how to show them. In my twenties, someone had to tell me that buying things for children was not the same as showing them love. In my thirties Jesus began to teach me how to love from my heart and not to be afraid of being unloved in return. He assured me that He would always love me.

I hated lesbians with a passion, not because they had hurt me, but in my eyes they all represented Dorothy.

I also tell those who have been affected by physical, verbal, or mental abuse a few simple things they can do to start the process of healing in their own lives:

1) Write down what you are afraid of facing, or tell someone you trust about what happened to you.

2) Realize that you will live through the pain you are feeling in your heart and chest as you accomplish step one. The pain will not kill you, and you can be sure that God is bigger than all the fear you have about facing this hurt from your past. It will take faith to believe at this point, but I guarantee God will see you through it.

3) Get some counseling. Look for an excellent Christian counselor, but try not to pick someone from your own church unless you're ready to have others find out about your past. You're going to need your own place of comfort and refuge. Your church should be your safe place during the battle being waged for your joy and healing. Try to find a professional counselor with a degree and check to see if she has some background in abuse counseling. Don't let just anyone use you as a test case.

Of course, the heart of my message and the beginning of all healing comes from a relationship with the Lord. None of my material would be effective without the power of the Holy Spirit working through me and in the lives of the people who are seeking help. It does not matter how long I live or teach, my healing will continue to be an on-going process, and now I'm thrilled there's more to come!

Chapter 21

Reflections and Projections

I have finally come to the point in my life where I've stopped blaming everything on Dorothy and have taken responsibility for my own actions. Even though I'm not pointing my finger in her direction, I can't deny her actions have had an adverse effect on my life.

The bottom line is that the seeds parents sow into a child's life do have a profound effect on them for the rest of their days. It doesn't matter how much parents love their children, or fail to love them, because children measure the words of their father or mother against their deeds.

Actions speak louder to the children than any rules and regulations parents design for them to live by. For instance, many of the men and women from my generation were instructed to stay away from alcohol. These same children would see their parents having a drink or two every day when dad came home, and on weekends they may have witnessed them passed out on sofas or in other degrading positions because of their over-use of liquor. Boys were told they should never cry, but they would often see their own father breaking down and crying under the influence of heavy drink. In a child's mind, contradictions like these only spell contempt for their parents and confusion for youngsters to endure and try to sort out.

This was certainly true in my life. When Cleophas left my mother, he lived with his mother. He slept upstairs, and sometimes when I went to see him, Grandmother Wright told me not to bother him. She made up excuses, that he had just come home from work and was tired, or he had to work late. Regardless of her efforts, I would always go upstairs after him hoping things would be different. However, before I got to the middle of the staircase, I could smell the booze and it literally reeked from his body even after he had bathed. Having him tell me not to drink would have been worthless dribble.

I'm grateful that I was turned off by the impression Cleophas burned in my mind, but many children end up following in their parent's footsteps even when they initially despised their actions. If the figures are correct, children born during and at the close of World War II had some of the highest numbers of alcoholics and this era produced many children who became heavy drinkers.

The truth is that eighty percent of what any child learns is "caught" rather than "taught." How could the confusing messages which were passed on through the blood lines in the past be any different from the message homosexual parents are sending to their children in this new century? Unfortunately, gay parents may even be openly encouraging their children to pattern after their own lifestyle.

In other ways, parents also send messages to their children that are simply the result of miscommunication. Until I was twenty years old, to my knowledge my father was in a constant state of drunkenness. When I was pregnant with Scott, he came out to see me in California. I was 27 years old at that time and I waited to see if he would pull out a liquor bottle and drink in front of my children. But by the time he left I was finally convinced that he was clean and sober.

I was happy for him and asked him when he had stopped drinking. His answer was, "The same year you left Pittsburgh." My first thought was, *I was the reason for his drinking. As soon as I left town, he was finally able to quit.* I was devastated by his response.

Now I realize that my actions had nothing to do with his alcoholism, but having come from a background where he was physically and emotionally absent from my life, it was very hard for me to grasp the proper meaning of his words at that time. Only in later years did I free myself from that unnecessary guilt. In his defense, I also learned that, the times he tried to be there for me, Dorothy wouldn't permit him to come around.

I mention this only to make the point again that everything we do, good or bad, will have an effect on our children. As a parent, I maintained a lot of inward rage, but because I kept my cool at home every day, I convinced myself I really didn't have anger issues. I was really shocked to learn the truth, and my first clue came as my two sons matured into adulthood.

Both Durksen and Scott had problems controlling their anger, and I certainly couldn't blame their fathers because they were never there to influence them. Of course, a part of me wanted to deny I had anything to do with their problems, but as I continued to seek counseling and faced my own inner conflicts, I discovered exactly where their problems were stemming from.

My children were never abused or beaten, nor did I curse them out or call them nasty names. However, they both had absentee fathers and the lack of a male presence in their lives hurt them deeply. All along I was trying to live a clean Christian life. I had no man living in my home so they never witnessed adults interacting in a relationship.

I was so busy trying not to live my life like Dorothy that I never stopped to think what I was passing on to my children. I didn't believe I deserved a husband, so I was unable to give my children the balanced life they needed and deserved. I deeply regret that!

It is true that both heterosexual and gay parents can put their children through some of the same issues. They can suffer the trauma of one of the parents leaving home. Overheard arguments and physical abuse often deeply affect the children's well-being. Any parent can expose their children to an excessive party life and drinking and drugs. In general, children today often have to deal with one or more of these problems.

However, children raised in homosexual homes have additional issues to sort through. Will they grow up and marry someone of their same gender? If their mother sleeps with women, will the little girls want to try to do this at an early age? Or, since dad kisses guys and brings them home to sleep with him, maybe that is what the boys should do? How can a parent help a child with gender identity problems when the kids see everything their mom or dad is doing with their same-sex partner?

In addition to these obvious concerns, most children raised by gay parents, including myself, have struggled with voyeurism. I believe this is because of the things they've heard coming from Mommy or Daddy's room, or the things other kids say concerning them that they heard from their parents. They have no idea if the information they hear about their caretakers is true or not because even though they live in the same house, they may not have seen all of the activities that they hear other people talking about. The children often end up trying to match the rumors with the sounds they hear coming from the master bedroom.

They may even try to see things for themselves. This is another area where the children become really confused.

The children's classmates or playmates usually report only what their mother or father has told them about the offending parents, and these words can be brutal. Although the children in homosexual homes love their parent figures, the ugly words people say about them and the way homosexuals live their lives will hurt the child and often cause them to become angry and bitter. Regardless of some new laws and programs designed to stamp out all prejudice that have been initiated in certain school systems, when children grow up in a gay home, they are going to be teased and made fun of no matter where they live.

In the same light, homosexual parents who think they can hide their behavior from their children are badly mistaken. If the truth doesn't come from the parents, it will surely come from other sources. No matter when the painful truth is revealed, children of lesbians will have problems relating to men and children of gay men will find it difficult to relate to women. They will not have had anyone to serve as a proper role model, and future relationships the child tries to develop will be in jeopardy until the child is able to sort through the facts.

Adults who have grown up in a homosexual home and identify with some of these issues should seek out professional Christian counselors to deal with all their underlying hurts and doubts. There is no shame in seeking help, and the benefits include feeling better about themselves and the quality of their life will begin to soar. They should never accept the lie psychologists and counselors have been known to give which says, "If you have any doubts about your sexuality, then you just need to lie down and accept the fact that you are a homosexual and you should stop trying to fight it." I say, "Fight it with the Lord's help!"

If teenagers are currently living in a homosexual home, they do have a choice. But they don't have to follow in the footsteps of their gay parent. They don't have to experiment with homosexuality or lesbianism just because it's the "in thing" to do these days.

Believe me, it's a trap and once they are caught in the grips of it, they will find it squeezing the life out of them. It has the power to remove all the traces of who they once were and it consumes their very souls.

Homosexuality is no game. If a person has not been raped, molested or verbally and emotionally assaulted, they should not attempt to play around with homosexuality as they would an experimental drug. They won't be able to take a hit today and walk away tomorrow. However, if people do get caught up in homosexuality, there is a way out if they desire it.

Children of homosexual parents should love their own flesh and blood, but again, they don't have to follow in their footsteps. They also don't have to believe all the mean things other children say about them. The temptation is to surrender your heart and give in to a life of anger, but anger is like a cancer and will literally eat you alive. Forgiveness can only come from the Heavenly Father.

Now I can honestly say that I have forgiven my mother and love her with all my heart. There is such joy and freedom in saying these words! The process of healing in my life has certainly not been a picnic. I've had to fight for it, but forgiveness has been the key to my wholeness. Today I'm in a better place than I was a year ago, and my future has no limits.

Although I've been in leadership, I continue to look to the Lord and fellow believers to correct me. Whenever I'm in a service where the speaker is on target with some problem I happen to be struggling with, or if an old wound rears up from time to time, I go up to the altar or get on my knees right there in the pew to allow God to do business with that stronghold.

My Heavenly Father doesn't want me to live with a stronghold of self pity on my life, and let me tell you, I've been guilty of that. God says in the Word that His grace is sufficient for me and He will give me beauty for ashes, the oil of joy for mourning and a garment of praise for the spirit of heaviness (Isaiah 61:3).

As a new believer I learned all of this by heart, but it took a while to learn how to put it into practice. Evangelist Tim Story once told the story about Paul and Silas being locked up in the jail at Philippi. They were in stocks and had been beaten thirty-nine times for going on a journey which God had directed them to take.

When midnight came, Paul and Silas began singing songs and praises to God. Tim pointed out that when Paul was squeezed tight enough, what came out of him were songs and praises to his God. When we are squeezed, what comes out? What came out of me in the past was self-pity and anger.

I would say, "What have I done to deserve this? Why hasn't God heard my cry for help? God must not love me anymore." When I was squeezed, I murmured and whined and felt really sorry for myself. What God desired of me is found in Proverbs 3:5-6. He wanted me to learn to trust in Him with my heart and not to lean on my own understanding of things.

I must trust Him when situations are looking very black and doubt looms its ugly head about everything God has directed me to do. Often, when I have obeyed something God has instructed me to do, doubt creeps in and causes me to crumble and fall apart. Later I get hit with a two-by-four as I decide on my own what I should do. The Lord tells us not to try to figure things out on our own, but to trust that He knows how to lead us.

My childhood left me with a lot of mistrust and fear, but God didn't intend for me to stay in that place. He takes care of the hurts of the past when we ask Him. We are like clay on the potter's wheel (Jeremiah 18). The Holy Spirit throws us on the wheel and molds us until we fit the shape and job we were designed to do. Before God takes us off the wheel, however, He must poke us with a wire to be sure all the air pockets are collapsed. All potters know an air pocket will cause the clay to crack and weaken.

In the past I had prayed, given tithes and offerings, and I still had no husband, no raise, and no ministry. After the air pocket check was complete, and God shaped me the way He desired, He put me on the shelf to dry. This meant I had to sit and wait for Him to call me. I had to become submissive to His plans and His timing, as well as the call He has placed on my life.

I've learned a lot from my past to help me understand the God I now serve. I realize God Himself chose Dorothy to be my mother and He knew what she would be like ahead of time. My life was no surprise to Him, and neither was hers. Psalms 103 and 139 assure me that God knew me even before Dorothy gave birth.

Yes, we have a choice, but God says in Psalm 139 that He knows my thoughts from afar and my words even before I speak them. He used Dorothy's womb to bring forth four children. The two I know are going about their Father's work until Jesus returns.

To borrow a line from Solomon in Ecclesiastes 12:13, "the conclusion of the matter is this": . . . it is sometimes hard to write the conclusion when one is still living and learning. In almost every emotional situation I encounter, I'm still learning how to process through it. Nevertheless, God's vision for my future is not yet complete, but I have joy in partaking of the ministry He has graciously created for me.

I also have clues of where the Lord would ask me to expand my work. Lately I've noticed many churches have boldly created ministries designed to help the adults involved in homosexuality. However, they still seem to be forgetting the children who are brought up and greatly affected by these adults. I have never heard of one program or read a book from any psychologist or counselor who has addressed the hurts, doubts, and fears a child faces when growing up in a homosexual environment, and I have been asking myself why.

I believe no one has yet acknowledged the fact that we hurt. I can attest that these children are in a degree of pain which extends into their adult lives, and no amount of denial from the homosexual community or any expert psychologist can change that fact. I personally would like to see this remedied, and I pray the telling of my story is a step in the right direction. Let my life be a living reminder that God has a special place in His heart for those whom have suffered as I have. He is using the hurt of my life as a healing light to others who are locked in strongholds of this very pain. Until the church is able to expand its ministries, I pray God will allow me to tell the children of homosexuals, both young and old, He wants them to be set free of their past and become the people they were designed to be.

I bring you tidings of great joy! I'm now confident that I will always be my Heavenly Father's little princess, and because of His great love for us, He will continue to heal and ultimately shape all of us into His image as long as we invite Him into our lives.

To God be the glory!